➤ AMIGAS ◄

Book Three

Louann Atkins Temple
Women & Culture Series

Books about
women and families
and their changing role
in society

University of Texas Press
Austin

AMIGAS

*Letters of
Friendship and Exile*

Marjorie Agosín and
Emma Sepúlveda

Translated by
Bridget M. Morgan

Publication of this book was made possible in part by support from
Allison, Doug, Taylor, and Andy Bacon; Margaret, Lawrence, Will,
John, and Annie Temple; Larry Temple; the Temple-Inland
Foundation; and the National Endowment for the Humanities.

♾ The paper used in this book meets the minimum requirements of
ANSI/NISO Z39.48-1992 (R1997) (Permanence of Paper).

Library of Congress Cataloging-in-Publication Data

Agosín, Marjorie.
Amigas : letters of friendship and exile / Marjorie Agosín and
Emma Sepúlveda ; translated by Bridget M. Morgan — 1st ed.
    p.   cm. — (Louann Atkins Temple women & culture series)
ISBN 0-292-70505-0 (cloth : alk. paper) — ISBN 0-292-70506-9
(pbk : alk. paper)
1. Agosín, Marjorie — Correspondence — Translations into English.
2. Sepúlveda-Pulvirenti, Emma — Correspondence — Translations
into English. 3. Authors, Chilean — 20th century — Correspondence.
4. Women authors, Chilean — Correspondence. I. Sepúlveda-
Pulvirenti, Emma. II. Title. III. Series.
PQ8098.1.G6 Z486 2001
861'.6409 — dc21
[B]   2001023071

Many people have contributed to our destinies as women and as immigrants. Their efforts have given us opportunities and inspiration. I dedicate this book to the professors who did not laugh at my accent and I thank them for their kindness. And to those who ridiculed me, I thank you for the strength and determination that you forced me to find within myself. Above all, I dedicate this book to Emma, *una verdadera amiga del alma,* a true friend, the kind encountered only once in a lifetime. Her friendship and faith have helped me become the person I am today. I am also grateful to my parents, my husband, and my children for their support. I especially wish to give a heartfelt thanks to Professor Richard A. Curry, who encouraged my growth as a poetess.

—*Marjorie Agosín*

These pages are an epistolary testimony of a path that has taken me across seas and lands, and through languages and beliefs, love and exile. I dedicate them now to the people who have journeyed with me and have taught me to celebrate life.

I thank María Elena and Helga, the friends of my infancy and childhood in Chile, for friendships that know neither borders nor distance.

I thank Nancy and Allyson, my friends in this land of the North, because they understand my dreams and believe, like me, that I still can change the world.

And to Marjorie, thank you for helping me decipher the mysteries of life through our letters.

I also dedicate these pages to the memory of my mother, Angela Pulvirenti Salinas, because she showed me how to seek happiness in times of sorrow.

And my thanks to John, for loving me in spite of everything.

—*Emma Sepúlveda*

ACKNOWLEDGMENTS

Our letters were transformed into a publishable manuscript through the help and cooperation of several people. Our most sincere thanks to Dr. Bridget "Tammy" Morgan for her painstaking translation and secretarial support, and to Dr. Darrell Lockhart for his revisions to the manuscript.

Many thanks to Theresa May for her dedication and patience during the long journey she has taken with our letters, embarking with the proposal of this project and finally arriving with the creation of this book.

—*Marjorie Agosín and Emma Sepúlveda*

and wore a bit of makeup, some of us with too much mascara layered on our lashes and our skin bronzed with the aid of a magical cream called Sunbeam. The more modest girls, or perhaps the most audacious, anointed their bodies with Coca-Cola, as I did.

Emma was a beautiful teenager with long, luxuriant black hair. My fine blond hair was shorter than hers. Suddenly we looked at each other, and it was with that glance that two similar beings discovered and recognized one another. I asked her, "How long have you been letting your hair grow?" She smiled and said, "And how long ago did you cut yours?"

In the story "Trenzas," María Luisa Bombal (that marvelous writer of our adolescence) says that hair symbolizes the intimacy of shared experiences. That encounter changed our lives; it was as if our tresses, dark and light, had become interwoven in order to exemplify the course of those lives.

Emma and I conversed, ate ice cream, confessed our lives and our loves in a few brief minutes, and promised to meet again the next day. I returned home that afternoon filled with the incredible happiness of having found a treasure and, above all, a friend who had not begun by asking me the question that had plagued my childhood: Are you Jewish or Chilean?

On the second day, Emma and I continued our conversation. She told me of her passion for history, her domineering father who had sent her to a school run by sinister nuns, and her mother who wept in dark rooms. I spoke to her of my family, peaceful beings, practiced readers. I told her how my mother and grandmother cried both when they received letters from Vienna and when they stopped receiving them.

Emma confessed that I was the first Jewish girl that she had ever really known. I asked her, "Does it surprise you that I don't have a big hooked nose? Or that I don't have horns?" She looked at me, then winked a dark, sparkling eye and kissed my head. That kiss meant so much to me. Promise, hope, revelation. We swore to each other, as young girls swear, to write to one another, to tell each other of our lives, and to be a mutual source of comfort throughout the years.

These letters, written over the course of more than thirty years, reflect our friendship, dreams, and concerns. In this collec-

AN OPEN LETTER TO OUR READERS

During the evening here in the Northern Hemisphere, I enjoy saying the names of the southern constellations aloud—las Tres Marías, las Tres Pascualas, la Osa Mayor—perhaps because enumerating the stars of my homeland reminds me of my sky and of my experiences, of a past that now has the same destiny as all dreams and memories.

The precariousness of memory, the ambiguity of remembering, along with our obsession for recalling the past have been a central part of our exile in the United States. My mother's final preparation for our journey was to pack hundreds of letters from her childhood into her handbag, correspondence from and to her dear friends, postcards from her family in Vienna. Beautiful letters written in an elegant hand. I could recognize only a few names of those distant cities—Vienna, Prague. We were uncertain if the addressees had passed away from old age or if they had died in the depraved chambers of blue gas. Nonetheless, that miraculous bag filled with graceful words confirmed our past and assured us that our ancestors would be with us at our new destination, North America.

In the same way that my mother managed to survive in distant Chile during World War II by treasuring the letters from her relatives as if they were priceless gems, the reader of this book will discover that this collection of letters written between the years 1965 and 2000 are the jewels of memories shared by two friends who are both similar and distinct, two friends united through their dreams of adolescence and their hope for justice and equality, friends who have chosen parallel pathways in the spiritual journey that they share.

I met Emma Sepúlveda in January 1965 during a steamy summer in the Southern Hemisphere. We encountered one another at the popular seaside resort El Quisco, located an hour's drive from Santiago. As was the custom in those days, the girls would stroll through a district known as El Melocotón. We dressed in white

tion we have chosen letters that we found most significant, beautiful, and memorable. Some of them are exactly as they were originally written. Others have been edited not only for greater clarity but also in order to emphasize what we as adults have found to be central to our lives. A few of the letters began as sentence fragments or paragraphs upon which we have elaborated.

Our purpose in this collection is not to reveal specific facts and exact dates. Thus several gaps exist in the chronology. The lack of letters during those gaps lays them bare, demonstrating that very often life, like history, cannot be measured by means of chronological events or concrete texts, but instead is measured by means of memories, instances that make an impression, that leave prints but yet allow our memory to flow freely. It is not our intention to reveal every intimate detail of our lives, but rather to permit the reader to view specifics that profoundly shaped our experiences.

We hope that those who read these pages imagine us as two travelers on parallel routes. Two writers—one of poetry, the other of prose—who communicate their truths through writing, through words. Our correspondence reveals the spaces in our lives. First appear the letters of our youth and our years in the university. Then the political situation that shook Chile in the seventies prompts a lapse in our correspondence. The letters begin again once both Emma and I relocate to the United States—Emma in Nevada and California, and I in Indiana and New England.

Our personal lives, the history of our marriages and children, do appear in our correspondence, but for us the experience that unites us and that we want to share with you is the experience of exile, of belonging neither in Chile nor in the United States—the experience of existing between two cultures and not feeling comfortable in either of them, of choosing the path of political activism, and uniting our destiny with that of other marginalized women.

We do not want this book to be a record of our personal afflictions. Rather we present it as a history shared by thousands of others of our generation. It is the history of those from the Southern Hemisphere who were forced into exile for the crime of being young and wanting to change the world. We are the fortunate ones, for we survived, thanks to the love that surrounded us and to our passionate struggle for social justice. The two of us are products of the sixties and seventies, which were perhaps the most marvelous and disastrous epochs in the history of Latin America. We attended schools and universities in order to change the world. We listened to Victor Jara and Violeta Parra until the early hours of the morning, and the world, the streets, and our city belonged to us. With the arrival of dictatorships to Chile, Argentina, and Uruguay, Emma and I would never be the same. We lost not only a country but the dream of an entire continent: our generation's dream.

We came to this other America in search of refuge and freedom, all the while knowing that the CIA had helped topple the government of Salvador Allende, someone we had admired and who now is reborn in the presidency of Ricardo Lagos.

Amigas represents and reflects our carefree years of long vacations at the beach and in the countryside. But that external, superfluous existence slowly gives way to an exploration of the most profound issues of our reality: social prejudice within the Chilean as well as the Argentine culture, discrimination against women, and the machismo that inundated our lives. These letters that we are sharing with you are our obsessions and our treasures. They are the clearest reflections, not only of our souls but also of the times in which we were fated to live.

Many times we have wondered why we survived, how it had been possible to bear our complex emotional burdens for dozens of years. The answer is simple. Our letters, the letters that you see here, are enchanted threads held in place by means of the words that we send one another for the purpose of sharing the lives stolen from us through events that stripped us of our souls, of the land of our memories, our language, and our precious identity.

These letters were written in Spanish. The reader will observe that the voices are transformed with the passing of the years. The translator has been faithful to their colloquial style. But, more important, she has sought to re-create in the English language our Latina reality, a reality submerged in the spaces of affection, passion, and memory.

Emma and I, I and Emma, have traveled down a long road. I

have let my hair grow and she has cut hers a little. My hair has darkened and gray has lightened hers. We have given birth to children, we have shared the dreams and fears of being Americans and foreigners, but we have essentially changed very little. We call one another frequently, two or three times a week. We begin our conversations in absolute seriousness, discussing university politics or human rights (for us, a constant topic), but quickly we begin to remember things we did in El Quisco, in Santiago, or in Reno, and we then know that we have returned home. We have returned to the familiar territory of a shared youth. Memories are no longer distant; on the contrary, we seem to have a magic flying carpet that carries us to the voices of our first encounters. With Emma, I can be Chilean-Jewish and gringa, all those identities together, and with me, she can be Catholic, agnostic, Chilean-Argentine, upper class, and popular. The friendship that exists between beings, a true friendship, should not judge but should be diaphanous and luminous. It should open the doors to understanding. As Violeta Parra sings in a song that Emma and I have heard together countless times, friendship should "alleviate the suffering of the soul." This is what our correspondence tries to alleviate, the suffering of the souls of two immigrant women in a society that accepts them and rejects them, but nevertheless permits them to tell their story.

—*Marjorie Agosín*

✳

My parents brought us to Chile from Argentina so that we could see the Pacific Ocean and meet our grandparents who lived in the south. We were going to spend an unforgettable vacation in a country of wonders and then return again to our toys, house, and Italian grandparents who had settled in Mendoza. "One month, only one, four weeks, you can count them on a single hand," my father said when we were on the plane to Santiago, Chile, in March 1957. We stayed those four weeks and many more, until my little fingers were unable to determine their number. Then my parents stopped talking about Argentina and, slowly, silence began to shroud our infantile, obsessive questions. They no longer spoke of going back, and we never returned to our toys or to the old house with red walls. We stopped being Argentines, like my mother, and from that moment we became Chilean tourists, travelers who visited my grandparents' country estate in Argentina once a year.

Almost a decade later, still lost in Wonderland, I found my friend Marjorie Agosín without looking for her, almost by accident, as happens with all the treasures that surprise us in life. From the first moment, our similarities brought us close together and our differences united us. Two adolescents, one Jewish and the other Catholic, both living the confusions of a society decayed because of its incomprehensible traditions . . . they meet, their lives merge in an unconditional friendship, and they forge parallel roads while carrying throughout the world—and through time—their backpacks heavy with thousands of memories.

Meeting young Marjorie was like penetrating the confines of another world. I had never known another human being who could talk more than me. I had never known another girl who invented stories and played with the contours of the real and the imaginary as well as Marjorie did (and still does). She had what I always dreamed of having, and I possessed what she longed to own. Or perhaps it was the reverse? I am not certain if it was because we wanted to have something else or to change what we had, but through our endless stories we felt united from the first moment we met.

I wrote to Marjorie on those days when life seemed full of hope, when the most pressing obligation I had was to get on my knees and pray, try not to chew the wafer after receiving communion, and obey the instructions of the Irish nuns. But I also wrote to her when I was confronted by the cruelty of a man who could do everything except learn how to be a father. I wrote her about the unyielding strength of my mother, who suffered more than anyone else I will ever meet, yet died truly giving thanks for her life. I would write to my friend Marjorie because by writing her, I would live. I not only survived those profoundly challenging years but, through the words of our letters, I was reborn. Every time I wrote I was reborn, again and again. I wrote in order to set down on paper my profound suffering, the pain that I used to imagine would leave my daily life if I could make the words that described it leave my pen. In those days, I thought that things that hurt you could be shed or dislodged, like shoes we had outgrown or useless baby teeth.

The years passed and the letters continued being sent from and received in all corners of the world. They always have been, and still are, letters. I have never been able to send a postcard to Marjorie. When I write to her I cannot jot down a few lines on paper . . . it has to be pages and pages. I dialogue with her in my imagination. More than writing to her, I talk to her with a pen in my hand. I allow the ink to draw images and illustrate moments, and I know with absolute certainty that Marjorie will decipher my drawings and understand my words.

Marjorie's letters always arrive to me on pastel papers, like the antique silks of her clothes, and scented with exotic perfumes like those one bathes in during nights of a full moon. . . . She always places a keepsake from the beaches of Chile, a bar in Paris, or a square in Prague into the envelope. Marjorie's letters, more than letters, are poems. But I have not found this strange, since for Marjorie life is a poem, and she lives it intensely, like the passionate poems that she writes.

The topics of our letters continued evolving along with the changing paths that Marjorie and I have followed. Roads parallel and distant, narrow and dark. Exile changed our lives, and our lives altered the words in our letters. The political situation in Chile forced us to seek the road to exile, and since that moment we have wandered another's land searching for a peaceful, tender encounter . . . with our adopted country as well as with the homeland of our earlier dreams. Amid the confusion, Marjorie is the lighthouse that draws me near, guides me, and transports me to Chile on dark, stormy days. But she is also the soft, calm earth that affirms my roots in the dry soil of this country in the North. And so in this eternal exile we two, hand in hand across the distance, find pleasure in life, suffer its disappointments, cheat death, and win battles that we have never learned how to lose.

These letters tell a lot, perhaps even more than I would have liked to have known about me before I depart on my final eternal journey, but I am convinced that they should be made public as a testimony of the life of women in Latin America, and of the Latina immigrants who live in the United States. The histories interwoven in our correspondence are not exceptions, they are the norm. These episodes from the lives of Marjorie and Emma are part of a voluminous tome of common histories that have been lived and continue to be lived by Latin American women, from our grandmothers to our daughters.

In the pages of this epistolary work about two friends who seem to have known one another always, there are letters that follow the passing of the years and obey a chronological order, but there are also long spaces of silence that separate events and places. As we were editing the book, we wanted to present a history broken into fragments, into moments that gave form to our lives, instead of merely making a sequence of letters that constantly came and went, across the continents, rhetorically asking questions that we have yet to fully answer.

Many years have passed since we first met and since that first letter I sent to a young Marjorie in Chile. Upon beginning the new millennium, I wrote again to Marjorie from Chile, this time from distant Patagonia. I realized as I was writing the letter that all those trips we've made throughout the years, all the times we have bid farewell to Chile, were rehearsals for the final chapter that we will have to write someday. Calm and resigned, I finally took my leave of that long, narrow land in the south and returned to the North knowing and accepting that a part of my heart never crossed the Andes, but rather remains eternally suspended above the confines of the Chilean sea. And the other part comes with me to continue life in this country that I now miss and deeply adore. It could not have been a coincidence that, while I was being processed through customs at the Los Angeles airport after returning from Chile in January 2000, the young Latino agent handed my passport back to me, fixed his dark eyes on mine, and, with a smile of complicity, said in perfect Spanish, "Bienvenida a su patria, Sra. Sepúlveda."

—*Emma Sepúlveda*

➤ AMIGAS ◄

July 7, 1965
Santiago, Chile

My dear friend Marjorie,

I hope this letter reaches you before you and your parents return to Chile. I miss you a lot and think you are incredibly lucky to be able to leave school in the middle of the term to travel. I have had it with this place!!!! My mother insists that Our Savior Preparatory is a fine school and that not only will I learn to be a "proper lady" and a "good Catholic" but also I'll be well prepared to enter the university when I finish the sixth year here.

I don't like the nuns at all. I don't know how I'll survive the next few years. We have to pray in the morning, before lunch, after we leave class in the afternoon, and before going home at five o'clock. The religion classes bore me because they always talk about the virgin who had a child without being with her husband, and that everything in life is a sin and if you don't behave you'll go to hell. I can't imagine that God is so mean that He punishes you if you don't do everything you're told to do at home and school. Sometimes the nuns are cruel, too. The week before vacation, Sister Perpetua (that is really her name—strange, isn't it?) made me stand up in front of the whole school and accused me of wearing makeup. She scrubbed my face with a disgusting sponge to make an example of me so that all the girls going to our school would learn to respect the "purity" of women. They do the same thing if the hem of your uniform is above your knees or you wear hairspray—girls like that are loose and indecent. Also, they won't let us talk to the boys that attend the school down the street . . . so every chance we get, we open the windows and throw notes to the boys who are walking by or those passing by in cars so that they'll stop and talk to us through the iron bars on the windows. I have never been to jail, but I imagine it's something like a Catholic girls' school. They treat us like prisoners, and every time we do something to make ourselves feel pretty they tell us that we're acting like easy, indecent women, that we're flirts, and that no man will want us as a wife.

It also bothers me that in school we never talk about poor people. All the girls here, their families have money. Next door to Our Savior Preparatory is a little school for poor children who can't pay for classes like we do—their patio is just dirt, and when it rains they have to play in the mud. I watch them through the windows because we aren't allowed to talk to them or play with them during our breaks because they're poor and live in the slums. In their school, boys and girls are together, I guess, because the nuns there don't care about them kissing each other in the bathroom. Instead of an expensive uniform they use a white apron. They also stay in class longer than we do because we never see them in the street when we're leaving. I have always wanted to meet those children and ask them if the nuns are as mean to them as they are to us. Sister Consolation (how about that name?) told me that those children don't learn as much as we do, and that they go to school only to learn how to write because in the places where people like them live they don't like to study. She says that we shouldn't play with them because they have lice and like to steal.

Yesterday I told one of my classmates that you were Jewish, and she asked me if you were a cheapskate and if you had a big nose. In school if one of the girls doesn't want to share something or doesn't want to spend any money, they call her a Jew. But don't worry or get insulted by what those idiots say because I think you're wonderful and I believe that we'll always be friends.

Hurry back to Chile because I have a lot more to tell you.

Emma

❋

February 1, 1966
San Rafael, Mendoza, Argentina

To my best friend,

How I wish you were here with me and my cousins, uncles, aunts, and grandparents! Our family has grown, like it does every year. Sometimes I think that my aunts deliberately make plans during the winter to have more children in the summer. My mother says that because we are half Italian and half Argentine, and Catholic, we have to have a lot of children and be good cooks.

This summer two of my aunts who are nuns have come from Buenos Aires to visit my "nono" and "nona" (that's what we call our grandparents). My cousin María Rosa and I follow them all over the house because we want to see if they'll take the cloth off their heads so we can find out if they shave their scalps. The two of them sleep in a room by themselves, separated from the rest of the family. María Rosa says that they have to sleep on hard wooden beds so they'll suffer and wear long black clothes so that no one will see their bodies because they have promised themselves to Christ. I don't understand why they entered a convent, they aren't ugly and I think they could have found good Italian husbands (those are the kind my nono likes).

On Sunday, more than a dozen members of my family went to mass. I believe that they took all the children to morning mass because it was Nona's birthday and we ought to begin the celebration with God's help. We arrived at the church very early in case someone needed to take confession. I can't stand that part because you have to sit in a wooden booth and talk to the priest about your sins. And if that isn't bad enough, you have to organize them according to venial and mortal sins, and that can be a little complicated if you don't know why you did what you did, that is, if you did it on purpose or by accident. It always makes me very embarrassed to talk about such megapersonal things with someone I don't know. The only thing that makes it better is when my cousin Petisa goes first, and María Rosa and I sit real close to the confession booth and listen to her sins! She told the priest the same things she always confesses—she French-kissed Patricio, touched herself in places she shouldn't and enjoyed it, and admitted she had lied to Uncle Raúl. After confession, the mass began and us kids (only the ones who had already had their first communion) and the women went to take communion. That's another thing I don't like because you have that piece of bread stuck between your tongue and the roof of your mouth, and you can't chew it (because it's the body of Christ) until it melts away. After enduring the pain in our knees, the hunger (because you can't eat or drink anything before taking communion), and resisting the temptation to laugh—which always happens while the fat priest is giving a sermon—my family went back to my nono's house to continue the celebration.

When we got back to their house in the country, the men started the fire for the barbecue, and the women put on their aprons and went straight to the kitchen. At these family celebrations, the servants don't cook. The women have to prove that they can make the best pasta, salads, and pastries. We older kids have to take care of our little cousins. I like that because after all these years, now that we're over thirteen, we can be the ones who pick on the little kids. This summer we had a contest to see which of them could eat the most bugs or worms without getting sick. The winners receive prizes like being able to sleep alone in a bed or two pieces of cake, luxuries hard to come by when you spend the summer with what seems like thousands of cousins who are constantly coming and going in our nono's house.

The food wasn't ready until three in the afternoon. We kids ate at the huge table in the kitchen and the adults ate in the dark dining room that always smells like Tanax spray (they keep it dark and filled with that insect repellent to keep away the mosquitoes because, according to Nono, they carry diseases that the dirty Argentines have). Every family that lives close to our nono's house brought their own maid so that when it came time to serve the meals to the children, the children who had their servant there got bigger helpings and those of us who came from Chile took what they gave us without complaining. We didn't say anything because if the servants got mad, they'd get back at us by giving us food we didn't like. As soon as they left us alone in the kitchen, we began trading food. Whatever you don't like, you give to someone else and they give you whatever they don't like. Like we always do, we gave everything that none of us liked to José, because he can eat like a pig for hours. When we were all happy with the trades and José couldn't eat any more, we quietly called the dogs and they finished off the rest. In this family, you can't leave anything on your plate because it's considered an insult to the cooks.

After hours of eating and drinking, Uncle Nucho took out his accordion and we all started to dance. Nona opened the dance with Nono, then the whole family joined in. There's something so special about this music, and even though my friends at school would make fun of me if they saw me dancing like this, I love dancing to these old songs. My favorite is the tarantella and I dance them with María Rosa. We always hope that someday we'll dance the tarantella with an Italian man with green eyes and olive complexion, who will put his arm around our waists and whisper marvelous things in our ears.

After dancing and eating until we couldn't move, it was time for the grandchildren to present our "talents" in front of the whole family. It is one of our family traditions that I still don't like. The littlest ones open the show with poems they learned in school or dance to the rhythm of some song that Auntie Coca and Uncle Nucho sing off-key. This year Nona's birthday show ended horribly. The family asked all the grandchildren to dance La Raspa. I'm not sure you know that dance, but in my family it's almost the national anthem. All the children jump and skip while my family circles around us clapping the rhythm . . . "Dance, dance, dance, *la raspa*, jump and prance . . . " And we did—until José threw up all the food that we had begged him to eat during our three-hour meal that afternoon! By the time we had cleaned up the floor and washed the clothes of those unlucky enough to have been near José, the party had been ruined for all of us. One of my family's favorite punishments is to send the young people to bed while it is still early. So our party ended at five o'clock, before the suffocating heat of the day had ended, with us sharing a little bed with the cousin we disliked the most so that we wouldn't stay awake chatting.

We older girls could hear the whispers and laughter of the boys in the next room who were congratulating José because he blamed the girls for giving him so much food. Because in this family I have to tell you that the males always win. They tell dirty jokes, they wear pants, they can climb trees, they can even sip some wine during dinner, and they're allowed to stay up later at night. Not us girls. When we ask [our parents] why they don't let us do the same things, they always answer us the same way:

6 "Sweetie, what would people say if we let you do the same things as boys!?" Marjorie, is your family as crazy as mine?

I hope you're enjoying the beach and if you have a few free minutes please write to me. The mail here is as bad as it is in Chile, so if you send me a letter in the next few weeks I'll receive it. But if you can't write it and send it to me soon, mail it to our address in Santiago.

I can't wait to see you. Have a good time and write me.

Emma

❋

April 12, 1966
Santiago

My dear friend Marjorie,

I'm so sorry you're not here and that I can't tell you in person or even over the phone about my classmate Pilar's awful tragedy. You know that Pilar was going out with an Argentine guy (who is also her cousin) and every year he comes here to Chile to spend summer vacation with her. This time, after Cristian had gone back to Argentina, Pilar began to feel ill and told us that she was "late," but also that she had *not* had sex with him. When she told us that she hadn't started her period, we were scared—but then she swore to us that she hadn't gone to bed with him, and we calmed down. We're sure that Pilar isn't the kind who would have sex before getting married. You know that in our school they pound it into our heads that if we're not virgins, no man will want to marry us (not even the man who takes our virginity!). But things got worse and Pilar began vomiting every day after lunch. Then she missed another period. I can't even describe how upset Gilda and I were. You know that I would never have relations with anyone unless I was madly in love with him because I believe doing THAT is something so special, and I only want to do it first on my wedding night with the man who I'll spend the rest of my life with because then it would be totally romantic. As well, you and I have already talked about the first time you do it . . . it probably hurts a lot and you bleed, and that scares me. But another reason is that my mother says that you always get pregnant the first time you do it, and if that happened to me my father would kill me (and the poor guy who slept with me!). Well, in short, I wouldn't do it, not ever. I'm Catholic and because of that I have to be a virgin when I get married or I can't wear a white dress.

In spite of everything I've told you about what I believe, now I'm confused and can't get over what happened to Pilar. Like I was saying, her period didn't come and all three of us decided to go to the doctor together. We went to Dr. Sarrat. He's the Turk who has been my family doctor for years. I talked with him and told him that Pilar didn't live in Santiago and she didn't have any relatives in the area—but I don't think the old man believed me. At three in the afternoon we went into his office, our teeth chattering like we were dying of cold. Pilar insisted that she hadn't had sex, but I don't think the doctor believed that either. After touching and pressing her belly, and asking her over and over again if she had gone to bed with Cristian, he told her that she had to bring a urine sample to the hospital in the morning. So the next day we all signed the absence register and got an excuse to arrive tardy to class, and left school. We must have been nuts . . . we didn't know what we were doing and we were scared out of our wits. We scurried along, as frightened as cats being chased by a dog. We went to Our Savior Hospital (which made things even worse because it was only a few blocks from our school and we were wearing our darned blue uniforms). They didn't tell us anything while we were there, only "thank you" and "good-bye," and we went back to school, scared to death. Two days later the doctor called Pilar (thank goodness her mother didn't answer the phone) and told her that she was pregnant. Can you imagine being only seventeen years old and pregnant? How can someone who has never had sex end up pregnant? It frightens me to even think about it.

The worst thing is that although we had heard that if you are pregnant you can get an abortion (my maid, María, told me that), the doctor told Pilar that it was against the law and they could put both Pilar and the doctor in jail if they find out that she had an

8　abortion. Pilar was very depressed for a while . . . she even said that perhaps it would be best if she killed herself because she could never tell Cristian's parents that she was pregnant, and she kept insisting that she hadn't gone to bed with him. And then Pilar's maid told us that she had had abortions with the help of a woman who lived in the Juan Antonio Rios neighborhood, a poor area of town. The maid said she would go there with us. That afternoon at four o'clock we took a taxi to go see the woman. The neighborhood was so poor. . . . I had never seen anything like it in my life. Gilda said that if we got out of the taxi, we would all be knifed. I began to think that Gilda was right, and my mother's words kept running through my mind: if you go into a poor neighborhood, you won't come out alive. Gilda, Pilar, and I were terrified, I can't even begin to describe it. But Pilar's maid told us to stay calm, and kept repeating that these people were just like us only they didn't have money or clothes or food, and they had a lot of children. The part about a lot of children I didn't understand. Why have so many children when you lived near ladies who performed cheap abortions? We told the taxi driver to wait for us even though we knew that it would cost a fortune.

While the taxi waited, we went into a shack that was made of old bits of wood and a roof made of sheet metal. The woman who opened the door said that she could help Pilar immediately. Pilar went with her through a dirty curtain into the next room. Meanwhile, Gilda and I listened in silence as the woman told Pilar to take off her panties and lie down on the table. We heard her say that she was going to put something in her so that "it" would happen the next day. Pilar was calm when she came out, and after we got back into the taxi she whispered that the woman had put a packet of parsley in the hole where our period comes from. The maid said it was so that she would bleed. The next day at school, Pilar began to have terrible stomach pains and said that her period had started. For the next hour I was a nervous wreck because Pilar went white as a sheet and the nun teaching the religion class wanted to send her to the infirmary. Pilar kept telling me that she thought she was dying. Gilda asked for permission to call Pilar's house, and she asked the maid to come pick us up in a taxi. We left class and got into the taxi that was waiting among the cars driven by our classmates' parents and servants. We gave the driver directions, but because of the rush hour traffic it took forever to arrive at the little house of the woman who does the abortions. When we arrived, the woman told Pilar that she was ready to take the baby out of her. Just like the day before, they went behind a curtain, and we heard the woman tell Pilar to take off her uniform and panties and get on the table. After a little while Pilar let loose some horrible screams, and the woman kept repeating to her that she has to bear it because it was her own fault for getting involved in the problems of grown-up women and now she has to stand the pain like an adult. Pilar's cries were so loud that we wanted to tell the woman to stop taking the baby because surely Pilar was going to die anyway. We couldn't keep waiting, doing nothing, and we went into the little room to help Pilar. The only thing that I remember is seeing Pilar who was a sickly green, and so much blood . . . blood on the floor, the table, and the woman's arms. I felt like vomiting and the room began to spin. I opened my eyes and I was on the floor. Gilda was holding my head in her hands and I still saw all that blood in front of me. I asked Gilda to help me out of there because I had to throw up. On the other side of the curtain there was a disgusting bathroom, buzzing with flies. The stench was so awful, I began to vomit as soon as I went in — retching on the floor and everywhere else that wasn't filthy. Still overcome by the terrible stench and my vomiting that wouldn't stop, I heard Pilar screaming, begging the woman to please stop putting things in her, please take her to the hospital because she was dying. I don't know how long the nightmare lasted. I only remember Gilda yelling at me to open my eyes and rinse my face because I had to pull myself together, we had to help Pilar.

Marjorie, I wish you could have been there to see and hear what happened that day. I believe that no woman should get pregnant if she is going to need an abortion, or maybe she shouldn't have sexual relations at all so that she'd never get pregnant. We finally took Pilar home. Her maid told us that she would give her some hot tea so that she could sleep until her parents arrived home. The next day she didn't come to school, and her mother called my mother to let us know that Pilar was in the hospital in critical condition, and Gilda and I were to blame. My mother and Gilda's mother came to school, and Gilda and I had to go to Sister Perpetua's office, where we were told that we were accomplices to a crime. We were told to name everyone who knew about the abortion before the police arrived. Gilda and I bawled and told them that Pilar's maid and we were the only ones who knew. My mother was furious and apologized to the nun and Pilar's mother. My mother shot me a look that said "when we get home you're going to get it!" Then the big-bellied priest took us to another office, where he asked us again if anyone else knew about the abortion. You can't imagine those hours I spent crying with Gilda. They finally decided that they weren't going to turn us over to the authorities as long as we promised never to breathe a word to anyone of what had happened . . . we could never tell anyone about Pilar's pregnancy or abortion. I was so ready to promise anything and sign whatever they wanted that when the nun wrote on a piece of paper that Gilda Gómez and Emma Sepúlveda promised "to never divulge the evil sins they've committed to any teachers, students or other persons associated or not associated with Our Savior Preparatory School," I signed it. My teeth were chattering and my hand was soaked with perspiration, but I signed what I consider to be the most important promise I've ever made in my life. If anyone finds out that I've told you, I swear they'll grab me and put me in jail, so please, please don't tell anyone about this (most of all your sister).

Pilar is still in the hospital. My mother says that she'll never be able to have children, and her parents have told her that she can't go out with Cristian anymore. At school we pray every day for her. Sister Perpetua announces over the PA system that we will now pray for Pilar Molina, who is recovering from a serious operation brought about due to "perotinitis" (I wonder what that is?). Well, I can only say that I am very sad and confused, and I don't know why women can't have an abortion, especially girls like us who get pregnant by accident. Why are we obliged to have children if we don't want to be mothers? Why do they punish us? Why is it we break the rules of the Church if we have sex or will be excommunicated if we have an abortion? How about the boys who go to bed with us and help make the baby? What happens to them? Gilda says that we have to follow the example of the Virgin Mary, but that men must have sexual experiences before getting married so that they know what to do on the wedding night.

You have no idea how confused we are by all this, especially because Pilar said that she didn't really do it—that it was on the outside and nothing else—and even with that she ended up pregnant.

The older we get the more complicated life becomes. Even more so if you're a woman and a Catholic and you attend a high school run by a bunch of self-righteous nuns like the ones here at Our Savior.

Emma

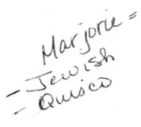

December 1966

Dear Emma,

I've finally found a bit of time to write to you. A few days ago we arrived in Quisco which, according to my mother, means "cactus," and a cactus, according to the Israelites, [is] very hard on the outside but sweet on the inside. As you know, in my home everything is "According to" and "Don't give up" and "God willing . . ." It's part of being Jewish. Everything is possible. One lives in constant conversation with God.

But now I want to tell you about this house that I already love, and hope that I never have to leave. My address is 152 Ejército Street. In the distance, one is able to just make out the ocean. Of course, it is not an imposing house because ours is, as my mother would say, an intellectual household. You know that we are fated to be intellectuals, because it would be unthinkable to say that one is a pure Jew but isn't an intellectual. Your mother and father came from the upper crust and we're descendants of humble, frugal tailors but, with God's help, my father managed to study and become a doctor, and so now we have this little house near the beach, fulfilling his dream to be middle class. From here, the ocean looks like a silvery little tail and one must imagine the rest of it. We mostly see the pines that are ever shifting and changing color according to the wind, the sea breeze, and the air currents. The house is made entirely of stone, and I love to press my cheek against its walls. I do that so I might feel sanctified—as if I were in one of those temples in which we can never worship because, as they tell us, we are Jewish and not redeemed.

I don't know why I tell you all these things, maybe it is because I can't say them to anyone else. Sometimes my grandmother warns us that we ought not to call attention to ourselves so that no one will recognize what we are and where we came from. Emma, you know all about the people in your family, about your aunts the nuns, and about your cousins. But I have always been terribly afraid of my ancestors; more than the unknown ghosts in the tales told by my nannies, I fear the spirits of all my relatives who died so far away and [lie] in neglected tombs.

I hope we will be happy in this new house at the beach. I believe we shall. My mother spends her time caring for the garden and she says that we will have good fortune because there are many lizards, and it makes me even happier to know that animals have come to live at our house. My room is very pretty. It doesn't look out to the sea but instead to a dense forest, secure and protective. I sleep in a big bed and pull down its large curtain, and once enclosed I am reminded of the tales from *The Arabian Nights*. I talk to myself and imagine myself to be one of the characters I create—almost all are princesses. I also play at being a widow or a single mother although I don't quite understand what that means, but the idea of being alone and being a mother appeals to me. I like to put that curtain between myself and the world. My mother laughs when I do this, but I know she understands me. When she was a child she wanted to be named Eugenia and not Frida, and she told everyone that her name was Eugenia. Do you think I could tell people that I am a princess? Of course, I would have to say that I am a Jewish princess.

Tomorrow I will have more to tell you because my relatives are coming to visit us in our new house. It's a short trip, but they're renting a van for the occasion. I don't know them very well, but I like my cousins. They're nice guys and very good-looking. I don't resemble them at all. They say that it's the mixture of Christians and Jews that improved the breed.

'Bye for now, Emma. I'm happy knowing that I will soon receive some news about your life.

Marjorie

February 1967

My dear Emma,

Summer is quickly coming to an end and my mother has begun to put the brocade covers on the furniture. At times, I see her with her head hung down, wondering about the fate of her beloved lizards. There is a devastating sadness to the end of certain seasons. I have packed away my white pants and I know that soon I will have to tie up my hair as the schoolteachers demand, but I wanted to let you know that this year I won't be going back to Union School. I know that you've had some problems at the nuns' school, but you can't imagine what it's like to be a Jew in an English Catholic—not even a Protestant—school. They look at you strangely, they spit on you, and they don't even try to hide their feelings. The most frightening episode was when my classmates made a circle, then they called to me and told me to get in the middle. I obeyed because I was always eager to join in their activities. So I accepted. I saw all of them with their white aprons and suddenly their faces went dark, became threatening, with me in the middle of them, and I felt the press of the group on my shoulders. There was nowhere I could run or hide as I heard them yell: "Who has stolen the bread from the oven?!" And the chorus responded, "The Jewish dog, the Jewish dog!" They said it slowly and I was deeply hurt, Emma, when I realized that, to them, I was that Jewish dog. They laughed at me because I hadn't had my first communion and my grandparents spoke with an accent. Emma, at that moment I wished I could leave Chile, to leave school, but where would I go? To what place, to which country, did I belong? Moreover, Emma, you know that I was born in the United States and everyone makes fun of me for that too. I cried all the way home. I walked the long blocks of Coventry Street until I arrived home where I saw my nanny, Carmencha, sweeping the sidewalk. I cried and asked her if she thought that we Jews were dogs. She only kissed me and I hugged her tightly. My mother then left very distraught and, that same afternoon, she took me out of that high school and enrolled me in the Hebrew Institute of Santiago. I probably tell you, more than anyone else, about these things that make me sad and ashamed because I have no one else to tell, and you've never made me feel different just because I don't have images of angels in my house, I only have an invisible God — and some dogs, but I do not know if they are Jewish.

Marjorie

✻

February 20, 1967
San Rafael, Mendoza, Argentina

My dearest friend,

Here we are again, spending the summer in Argentina with my cousins, aunts (including the nuns, who are also on vacation), uncles, and grandparents. I like to come back here because I feel that part of who I am is in this countryside, in my grandfather Silvestre's farm, and in María Rosa, who is my sister in the truest sense of the word (although we are really cousins). My mother had thought about us living permanently in Argentina, but we legally cannot do that without my father's permission. A couple of nights ago while the adults were conversing in the dining room, María Rosa and I decided to eavesdrop because we heard my mother and two of my aunts arguing loudly. Apparently, my mother had told them that my father had a mistress, another "home," and a son. As you know, in

Chile when you get married it's forever, so now that my father has another woman and children he has to decide if he's going to live with her, or live with his wife and her at the same time. That's what we call a divorce because permanently separating from your wife and marrying another woman doesn't exist in Chile, or Argentina either. That night, they said my father was a disgrace, that my mother ought to take the children and come live in Argentina, and the family would take care of us. My mother insisted that she still loved her husband and we shouldn't be raised without a father. She felt she could keep fighting and that he'd change and leave his mistress—after all, the poor thing had been in this situation before with other men (although my father was the first with whom she had conceived a child). María Rosa wanted us to continue listening, but I was very confused by how they talked about my father. On the one hand, it made me sad and ashamed when I found out that everyone knew about my father's lovers but I also wanted my mother to say yes, and we would come live in Argentina and our troubled life in Chile would end. I wished my mother would confide in her sisters and tell them what my father was really like. I wanted her to tell them that my father was always hitting her, and a few months ago he tried to kill her with a pistol but the gun hadn't fired. I prayed that she'd tell them about how he was always hitting us for whatever reason, especially me, because I'm the most rebellious in my family. I hoped she'd tell them how he punched me as if I were a man, a big man. He would throw punches at me and kick me, he hit me so that the pain would teach me to not answer back, to have good manners, to study, to eat, to go to sleep early, to arrive home on time, and everything else that he thinks a woman should learn by the rod. But my mother said nothing, she only cried and kept repeating that my father was the only man in her life and, although they were having problems, deep down he was a good father and husband. I couldn't sleep that night, and María Rosa and I talked for a long time underneath the sheet of the narrow bed that we shared. She said that it would be wonderful if we could come live in Argentina and end the suffering of my mother and the children. We both knew that it was only a dream because every summer when we came to visit, my father had to give us permission in front of a notary public, declaring where we would be and how long we would be out of the country on vacation. I find it hard to understand why my father doesn't want to live with my mother, but then I also don't understand why he doesn't want her to leave and take us with her. When they fight at home, Father always says that we're really my mother's responsibility and he only has to give her money to support us. Sometimes I'm terrified by the thought of what we will do if he stops giving us money, or if during a vicious fight he kills my mother and we're left alone.

Ever since I overheard that conversation, this vacation has changed. I don't want to go back to Chile and live with my father, but we can't stay here because my mother says that everyone looks down on a single woman with children and they think she is immoral—they say that her husband must have had a good reason to leave her because, if she were a good woman, her husband would still be with her. Marjorie, you know that it's always the same when it comes to being a woman: she's to blame for everything, the woman always suffers when her husband abandons her for another and leaves her with the children. I think I'm never going to marry, and if I do marry it will be with an old man who won't hit me and won't fall in love with a younger woman. But although I might marry an old man (maybe even thirty years old!), I promise you that I'll follow my mother's advice—study, study, and study so that I never have to depend on a man.

I'll write to you again in a few days. We won't return (that is, *if* we return) to Chile until March when school begins again.

Emma

My dear friend Marjorie,

Everyone is napping now to escape the terrible heat and also recuperate from last night's New Year's celebration. Our house was full of relatives and friends from Santiago. My brothers and I are allowed to invite our best friends to celebrate with us. This year I asked my neighbor Isabel, my sister brought her friend Ximena, and my brother, as always, came with Enrique because those two are inseparable. Last night we all stayed up late lighting fireworks, and singing and playing guitar while seated around the bonfire. The night was crystal clear and the stars shone brighter than ever before. When we stopped singing, we could hear [the] sound of crickets and dogs barking in the tenants' houses in the distance. At eleven, when the pigs had been well roasted over the heat of the coals, they called us in to eat and we took our seats at long, narrow tables that always remind me of those in "The Last Supper." We ate until we couldn't stand up. To my mother, the greatest insult is if guests don't eat up absolutely all the food that she prepares. I nearly die from embarrassment whenever she tells my cousins and friends that if they don't want to eat any more it must be because they don't like her cooking. This side of my family is as irrational as that in Argentina!!

A few minutes before midnight, Mamá ordered everyone to leave the table and prepare themselves for the New Year. You can imagine the commotion as dozens of people—old, young, even little children—rushed to be ready according to our family's traditions and superstitions. Before returning to the front room where we would all gather, we women went to our rooms to put on a new pair of yellow panties to bring good luck during the New Year while the men put on anything new . . . socks, pants, a belt, whatever, as long as it was being used for the first time that night. As the clock was ready to strike twelve, we each had to stand next to

18   a person of the opposite sex so that the first hug of the New Year would bring good luck. Afterward, you had to go to Mamá so she could give you a spoonful of cooked lentils so that you would be prosperous during the upcoming year and, after that, as always happens, some of my aunts and my mother began to cry remembering all our dead relatives who could not celebrate this New Year with us. The men laughed and hugged and toasted each other with another glass of their favorite cold spiked coffee called *cola de mono*. After the celebration ended and we had finished hugging one another in the living room, I went to the kitchen and gave the last hug to María, the servant we had brought from Santiago. All the maids and cooks who worked in the house were in the kitchen along with the nannies that my aunts always bring with them from the city to look after the children during parties. I have never understood why the servants have to stay in the kitchen as if they're something we're hiding from our guests or why they may only eat leftovers after we have finished eating.

The rest of the night was fabulous! The adults always go to bed once they eat and drink until they can't hold another mouthful, and then the nannies quickly put all the kids to bed so they can be free from their responsibilities. As happens every New Year, we young adults between the ages of fifteen and twenty were absolutely free the rest of the night to do whatever we wanted. We sang and danced until the sun came out at dawn, and some of us kissed in secret. I will have to tell you the details later because I'm sending this letter with my sister and I'm sure she will read it before putting it in the mailbox.

Thousands of kisses,
Emma

January 1968

Dear Emma,

I have not yet described how we spend the afternoons here on the coast. Well, after returning home from the beach—enveloped in a delicious warmth that leaves you drowsy and filled with a luscious thirst, so that it seems your body can feel happiness resting on its skin—we have lunch and take a wonderful nap. Since my father only comes home on the weekends, I often sleep in my parents' room, which looks out on the forest, and I especially love to be beside my mother to smell her because she smells like . . . like *Mamá*. I'm not sure if it's the scent of lilies or patchouli, but I love it, and I like when she tells me stories, like about how she spent entire nights dreaming about the love letters my father sent her and how she then saved them in a blue box, the color of a blue sky, of water. I don't want you to imagine that they lived far apart, because they lived in the same house, but they lived their love as if they were in a Jeannette MacDonald movie or other romantic movies they've let me watch . . . like those with Marcello Mastroianni. Oh, Emma, speaking of movies, I don't know if I told you something marvelous—my mother let me see *Gone With the Wind*. It was tremendous, and I liked Scarlett because she was somewhat bad, and you'll have to admit, Emma, that sometimes it's more fun to be bad than good. My mother was very mischievous. She put lipstick on me, padded my bra, and made me up with some face powder—not just rice powder but some made by Max Factor that she bought in the United States during one of those trips she makes to Miami every two years. She gave some money to the usher and we went in. I cannot begin to express how fascinated I was by that wonderful story that seemed similar to those I'm forced to endure at school during Purim.

Let me return to my description of our days here in Quisco. After our nap, we awaken thinking about tea time. There's nothing more exquisite than waking up and imagining what we will or won't have to eat—for us, teatime is no trifling matter. We drink a marvelous tea, and eat breads with *dulce de leche* and a large assortment of jams and jellies. Well, we are exactly like the people in Mendoza, don't you think? It's ridiculous to act so English when the truth is that we're such a damned silly little country. We want to enjoy our "eleven o'clock tea," so we even call it *las once*. Of course, during teatime I must have my favorite bun with pigs feet. In my house, we're naughty when it comes to pork . . . and we even put up Christmas trees. After teatime we go for a walk.

Quite often we go to a mysterious, secluded spot that is very near a large beach. We walk through a dense forest and great stands of eucalyptus. Often we sing or my mother plays guessing games with us, but mostly we do nothing but walk arm-in-arm. That is the most beautiful part of our walk. We make our way to what we call the Princess Rock. It is an immense rock that appears to have been carved with the faces of a prince and princess who are in love and are gazing at each other, both very happy and peaceful. My mother says that it is their rock because the lovers' families attempted to separate them and, so as to never be apart, they threw themselves into the sea. Their faces remained, sculpted in the rock. I love to listen to my mother tell stories. Her voice is soft like a velvet basket while her violet eyes change color.

I want to tell you of another of my wonderful walks. Well, I very much like to visit my father's friend Dr. Brodsky. I don't know why, but I feel a little tickling, like a butterfly, when I'm near Pablo, his oldest son. He shows me fascinating photos of the Cuban Revolution and of Che Guevara. He also talks about the Berlin Wall. My mother, nonchalantly, says that they have been communists for many years.

Well, those are my days on the coast. We return home, feeling like the heat has diluted our forms but nonetheless we walk along feeling happy and blissful. Afterward, we sleep deeply and only to you do I confess that I dream about being a princess.

Marjorie

March 1968

My dear Emma,

Today is one of the most thrilling as well as one of the saddest days of my life. I have a knot in my throat . . . and you are traveling through Argentina, discovering the secret of the nuns in your family. Do they know that I am Jewish? Do you believe they would have compassion for me or would they oblige me to confess that we were Christ's murderers and we still drink his blood? I am certain you always understood the way I felt whenever I heard my former classmates at Union School say: "You are the murderers of Christ." I would look at my hands and they would be clean, and I would wonder why I would kill such a good man who was, furthermore, a Jew? But this is not what I wanted to tell you. It is something else: Carmencita's departure. Emma, only a few minutes ago my Carmencita Carrasco left us, my nanny who brought us immense gray woolen blankets every summer because, as she would tell me, "Little daughter, one can be very cool on the inside." My Carmencha has gone, my *nana* who told me stories next to the gentle warmth of the wood stove while my pale fingers were entangled with her dark ones. I don't know how to speak to you about her. I believe she has always been here, ever since my mother was a coquettish teenager and Carmen protected the adolescent's secrets of love: wearing lipstick, the light in her eyes, the evening walks through the plaza on the arms of men wearing enormous blue capes (the cadets that she so adored!).

I now cannot remember who told me those stories—if it was she, if those are my mother's memories, or if they are mine. But she has returned to the south to die. She disobeyed the doctor's orders and with her fragile vessel has chosen a life of risk, a life overflowing with plenty, and simply left for the countryside, to her south, where one is unable to distinguish one day from another, where the afternoons are a violet hue and the sky is an orange blanket traversed by familiar stars. She left with her timeworn sewing machine, her shawl, and her guitar.

She went away, Emma, in a buckboard, thus crossing the modern and polluted city of Santiago. She left in a wagon with an orchid in her hair, a tape measure hung around her neck and a talisman made from pieces of potato at her temples. She departed as she arrived to our house: eccentric, half crazy and bizarre, but always *she*, magnificent, luminous, wise Carmen Carrasco Espíndola, the illuminated woman. The "Fortune Teller of the South," because that's what she liked to call herself, always desperately searching for imperious titles. She did not do this because of vanity but rather as a passion.

I have to tell you about her because my throat, my lips, and my thoughts are filled with bubbles and smoke. My Carmencita is leaving, my past, my imagination, the luminous angel of my childhood and the protector of my dreams. I know that you will believe me when I tell you that, dear Emma, on nights when my parents were not home, she would come to the room that I shared with my sister, sit at the foot of our beds, and sing beautiful hymns in strange and sacred languages until we were falling asleep . . . then she'd lightly descend toward us and would trace the sign of the cross and the star on our foreheads. And I blinked happily before her, my angel of all sweet dreams.

I do not know how to tell you about her. Words fail me about my pain, my grief. Now she has left and I have lost a little piece of Chile. I am desperate that I might lose my Chile in which I now feel I truly belong because — despite the time when she had to confirm that we didn't have horns — it was she who never made me feel like a foreigner, alone or different. Emma, my Carmencha has left me in her rickety buckboard, bound for the mountains. I foresee that this will be a land of farewells, one after another. I will never be a Simón Bolívar, I will always tread the soil of my homeland as a visitor to whom the right to belong is denied. Carmencita was my voice and my anchor, and now nobody will wrap me in gray blankets in the middle of the summer nor tell me tales of leprosariums and men who awoke each morning to await a possible love letter.

Dear Emma, have you had nannies like my Carmencita? All I think of now is a woman with the hair of a fairy, floating through the avenues of a silent city. I dream only about my Carmencha and I see her growing more distant like a chimera in a wagon with violet-colored wings, in a cart full of live and dead chickens, cures for lovesickness, and the music of a sewing machine that will never sew again. I confess only to you that she gave me a tape measure and bits of cloth filled with lavender.

Marjorie

September 1968
Santiago, Chile

My dear friend,

I am dying for this school year to end so I can enter the university, but at the same time I'm afraid to abandon the walls that have protected me for twelve years. I feel as if I have lived in a cloister of nuns . . . yet I also know that this cloister has safeguarded me from dangers I would have faced. The reality is that I am — no, *we* are — leaving this school and will begin a new life in a world about which we have been taught so little.

These last few days have been full of "illustrious moments" for all of us (to quote the old bat who teaches history). For me, it has been especially difficult for many reasons. My classmates voted me the prettiest of our class and I represented the sixth-year class in our school beauty competition. Marjorie, I was completely humiliated the moment I found out because I have always felt ugly, skinny, and clumsy. When they began to read the votes, each vote in my favor felt like a blow, and I would cringe. At first, I thought that it was a collective prank being played on me by the whole class! But afterward I realized that these girls who had shared twelve years of school with me would not be so cruel, and they wouldn't vote for me without good reason. I know I am a very good person and get along well with our younger classmates, and I can also be a clown when the occasion arises. . . . I believe that those qualities helped me win the first round. For weeks we had to sell votes to what seemed like half the world in order to win the school "crown." Some of the favorite places to sell votes were on the streets near the school. Since earning money for the school was the most important goal, the nuns lifted their restrictions and we were at liberty to stop cars filled with young men, then we would sell them votes any way we could. Once a car stopped, I knew they would ask me a series of questions to find out if I deserved to be crowned the "beauty queen": Let's see what you look like, turn

24 around . . . do you have a good-looking ass? Are you dating any-one? How old are you? I was also showered with unexpected comments like: "You don't have anything worth looking at in front or behind." "Your boobs aren't big enough." "You're scrawny, your legs are too skinny and your butt is too wide!" "You have a lousy figure." "Your face isn't pretty enough to be a beauty queen." "If you let me cop a feel I'll buy some votes." "Give me a kiss and I'll give you money." "Give me your phone number and I'll support you." This is how I spent hours raising money, feeling more like a prostitute than a contestant in a beauty pageant.

Finally, Saturday arrived and it was time for the coronation party. My father had purchased a lot of votes to ensure that I would win, and my classmates had raised money for a beautiful coronation ceremony, but I still felt that I didn't deserve it. I felt a little insecure about possessing the qualities of a queen, but I was absolutely panic-stricken at the thought of having to get on stage, accept the crown, and give a speech in front of all those people who would be thinking (like the men in the cars) that I didn't have a good ass or big tits (very important qualities for a woman who wants to be a queen, right?). Not only do I *not* have any curves and I'm as thin as a coatrack, I have hundreds of zits that have sprouted out of every pore on my face. And I'm still wearing these braces I've been stuck in forever so I can't close my mouth or open it all the way, and I spit when I talk. Because of all that, I convinced Camilo (I'm still going out with him) to go along with a plan I thought up, and we put the money I raised into the container of the other contestant from the sixth year. Then I slipped away from the party while my parents and friends weren't looking, still wearing the white lace dress that my mother had made for me (which was more fitting for a girl taking her first communion than for a beauty queen).

Marjorie, I consider what I did as an act of class spirit (because Teresa truly wanted to be queen!). Of course, it was also inspired by my fear of being ridiculed. When we returned home, what I had done gave my father a reason to start an argument that ended with the beating he always gives me. He came into the living room and asked Camilo to leave. He grabbed me by the arm

AMIGAS

and took me to my bedroom where he hit me so hard on my face that I was thrown to the floor between the nightstand and the bed. It was difficult, but I finally stood up and immediately fell down as the second blow hit me on the chest, and then he kept kicking me all over my body so that I couldn't stand up again. My mother and brother and sister didn't dare enter my room because they knew that when my father loses control, there's no reasoning with him. The only thing he said to me when he finally stopped hitting me was that I have to learn to be responsible in life. Then he left my room and I heard the door slam as he left the house. My mother came into my room and helped me off the floor. She was crying as she told me that, although I might not believe it, during times like these my father loved us and this was the way he knew how to teach his children because that was the way he had been taught. I hurt all over and could only think about going to the hospital because I was certain I had a broken bone, if not in my face where the bruises and welts were swelling up, then at least in my legs or all the other places where I'd been punched or kicked. My mother helped me into bed and said that we couldn't go to the hospital, and that I shouldn't tell anyone what happened because these are family problems and aren't anybody else's business. The truth is that my mother is afraid of my father and will never do anything to stop his abuse.

This is the way my path to the throne ended, without a crown and covered with bruises that prevented me from going to school for a week. When I returned to school, my classmates were furious with me and no one could understand why I didn't want to be queen. Meanwhile, I spent days explaining that my injuries were the result of a bicycle accident and lying, something my siblings and I have done so many other times because nobody dared remove the mask from such an honest, good, and caring man like my father.

Marjorie, my dear friend, I am now anxiously awaiting for spring break so I can begin studying for entrance exams so I can go to the university and be free of my father's bullying.

Emma

January 1969
Viña del Mar

My dear Emma,

I am writing both to console you and somewhat congratulate you for your recent experience as a candidate for beauty queen. I'm not sure how to say this, but I certainly believe that you are very pretty, the prettiest woman that I have ever met. I do not say that because of your face or your eyes, but for who you are and will be. I have never been a contestant in a beauty contest because I am very short and I have squat, fat legs and, of course, a bulbous nose. I have always wondered what it might be like to be tall and slender, and have a nose like yours—an aristocratic nose instead of one like an Irish nun! The first time I heard something about beauty competitions, they had to do with what the older people called "matters of political urgency." The truth is that politics has become an illness because for whatever reason people say, "He had to become a politician" or "It happened to him, that is, the vice of politics has taken him." Do you know that the word "politics" comes from Greek? A teacher told me, one that I adored because she was as fanciful and imaginative as I am.

Well, Emma, I have an aunt who is a little daft, unhinged, very odd in her madness. My mother says that she doesn't have any *zejel*. That means intelligence in Yiddish. But even more, as my mother puts it, she has outbursts of lucidity because she sings in Araucanian to the dead and she speaks to the servants in Yiddish. Well, it is this aunt whom I love the most because since I was a child she has known how to love me, listening to the wild yarns I would invent and now I don't remember. She is the one who participated in a beauty contest in her small county of Osorno.

Aunt Lucha was very beautiful ever since she was quite young, and had a memorable figure—not like today's models who need a corset to distinguish their fronts from their backsides. That's what Uncle Isaak used to tell us. Aunt Lucha wore red velvet dresses that matched her unruly, flame-red hair. One day her father, my uncle Isaak, decided that she should compete in the beauty contest of 1939. As you know, my mother lived with my grandparents in Osorno and she still weeps when she talks about the period that she calls the dark years of the war. Our entire life is divided into the years before and the years after World War II. Although Chile is very far from Europe, it was also involved in the history of Hitler and Nazism. My Aunt Lucha entered the beauty competition for Spring Queen. She was the only Jew who participated. The Socialist Party voted for her and so did the "Turkish" and Arab businessmen, because in Chile they call anyone of Arab descent "Turks." The Germans launched a fierce boycott. They stood at the kiosks protesting because "that Jewish dog" had entered the competition and they swore to burn down her house. They shouted at her, like they shouted at me years later in Union High School. Do you remember? Her German classmates were ready to stone her, and so goes her story of beauty, power, and triumph.

That Saturday night in the florid south, her fate was decided. My Aunt Lucha won the competition and was crowned Spring Queen. Like so many stories of Jews, and of those who are not Jews, in spite of misfortune there is a happy end.

Emma, congratulations. You deserve it for being the beautiful person and good friend that you are. I send you all my love. I know that you will triumph through your strength of spirit. I love you as one loves a big whale: A LOT, A LOT!

Marjorie

❋

February 1969

Dear Emma,

I received your last letter from Mendoza. My mother says that there the wines are exquisite and perfumed like the body of a woman in love. Have you tasted wine? If you have tried it, have you anointed it on your palate? I must tell you that once I saw my mother tipsy—her lips kept drinking deeply from a glass of wine until she became more and more happy and flushed. I saw her little by little tremble, blush, become suffused with emotion and then, enamored of her own glow, she laughed. Has this happened to you? I would like to know if you have tasted alcohol at some time. I admit that I have, not in the company of my parents but instead with the nanny that we have now. We all love her very much but not on the nights when, as they say, the vice of alcohol enters her veins. My mother says that she is named María like all Christian females. Have you by chance known an Indian named María or a Christian called Rebecca? Well, these are small parentheses in this story about drinking that I want to tell you.

One Sunday, my parents were taking a nap with their bedroom door closed. María said that they weren't sleeping, that they were doing things of love, playing games and moaning. So she said. That left me confused because I didn't understand much of what she meant, the same as I don't understand much when they talk to me about single mothers. But in short, that afternoon we went to town to walk through the sunny streets filled with dust, unconcerned. We arrived at a small, sleazy tavern where both the drunkards and the dogs were yawning. The place was called the Comfort, and there María told us that she would give us a drink that is like golden foam on your lips. So it was. She gave us some plastic cups filled with a very yellow, thick liquid. My sister and I eagerly tried it and quickly abandoned it. María drank and drank until she laughed madly or cried desperately. She told me that she loved the scent of drink and that it made her feel happy inside. Poor María. Always talking to herself, singing alone, and meeting strange men in the afternoons, who whistled at her and she would go to them, hypnotized by their calls.

It was after dark when we arrived home and my panic-stricken parents and the police were in the street looking for us. María staggered inside and we followed, happy and only concerned because we had found glowworms on the path. So, Emma, that was my first contact with the bubbly liquid that I now know is called beer. Since that day, more than just alcohol, I am intrigued by forbidden things.

AMIGAS

I like to watch adults whispering in each others' ears and saying things that make them blush deeply. Someday I will understand what it means when they talk of "bubbles of love," but I shouldn't be in a hurry. So says my mother. I should live without rushing myself because soon and without wanting to I will be a woman. I only want to be a woman who writes. And you, Emma, what do you want to be when you are grown up? Would you like to take photographs? Or be an opera singer . . . or simply contemplate your ankles for hours?

Marjorie

❋

April 1969
La Serena, Chile

Dear friend,

I still don't believe it but my dream of attending a university far from my home and my father has come true. As I told you before, I applied to several cities and to all the universities that would require me to leave Santiago. The names of the students accepted to the University of Chile and the Catholic University of Santiago were published in our local newspaper *El Mercurio,* and my name did not appear on the list because I hadn't applied to any universities in Santiago. My father accused me of not having scored well enough on the Academic Aptitude Test to enter the two most important universities in our country (according to him!) and my only defense was my customary silence. A few weeks later they published the lists of the universities in the provinces and my name appeared on some of them. My father, caught off guard, immediately declared open and vicious war against me, did battle with words . . . and blows when I defended myself during our heated arguments. After threatening me hundreds of times with "you are going away but I'm not giving you a goddamned cent," my parents decided that they would permit me to live far from home under strict conditions, which I had to swear

30 to accept while I held both hands on the Bible. The conditions were that I would have to live in a boardinghouse of "young ladies" where there was a strict curfew, a *pensión de señoritas* that prohibited the visits of men and unknown females, and where the owner would make weekly contact with the parents of the "young ladies" who roomed there. After accepting those conditions, I left en route to La Serena accompanied by my father and mother. I hadn't the remotest idea where the city was, what it was like, or what kind of university I would find. Only two things were clear in my mind: I was leaving my father's control and La Serena was near the sea—the two dreams that had shimmered brilliantly on my lonely horizon shone more intensely now than ever.

We spent two days in a hotel and then my parents left me settled in the boardinghouse of a widow who has the same characteristics as Sister Perpetua, but with two differences: she never feeds us enough so that we will "keep our figures" and she turns off the lights at nine o'clock so that we get enough sleep in order to prevent wrinkles. The two rules have been undermined by the girls who have been here for some time—they hide food under their beds and they light candles after the old lady turns off the lights. Hiding food worries me because the rooms are full of ants and they get into our beds. There is no access to the bathroom at night so we need to be careful not to drink anything before going to bed, or to eat watermelon with toasted grain, because we would have to use the little chamber pots that are kept under some of our beds (stored between the heavenly snacks that we are going to eat the following day). I can't begin to tell you how we suffer when we need to urinate in the middle of the night. First, you hold it until your bladder almost explodes, then you get up as carefully as possible so you won't step on too many cockroaches and you feel around under the bed until you find the little metal pan . . . which by that time of night has already been pissed in by some of the other desperate girls who weren't able to contain themselves. After "locating the treasure," usually almost overflowing with pee (and you've probably already stuck your hand wrist-deep in piss to find it), you very carefully slide it out from under the bed and, in the darkness, try to aim your stream directly at the middle of the chamberpot. The first few times I felt terribly guilty when I didn't hit the target, but now I have realized that my fellow nocturnal piddlers have the same problem with missing (or pissing) because beside the beds where the pans are kept the floor is always soaking wet. The windows are covered with iron bars like in my former Catholic school so that (according to the widow) no one can enter to rob us. But I personally believe that it is so that those of us who have boyfriends won't sneak them in through a window. On Friday and Saturday nights, those who have dates are helped to escape. Some of us keep watch in front of the widow's bedroom door and others light the fugitives' path to the patio with lanterns. Then, once there, we push them as best we can over the wall to the street while one of us is feeding sugar to the damned dog so it won't bark. The work is exhausting because then at dawn, when they tap on the window, we have to sneak out again in silent teams and repeat the process with the dog, look for the girls over the patio wall, and pick them up off the ground after their boyfriends catapult them, by means of a fierce shove, into the middle of the patio between the papaya trees.

Life here in the "ladies' boardinghouse" has been a hard and complicated experience for me because I am the youngest of a group of women who have lived in surroundings very different than my own. Some of them are millionaires and are only studying to please their parents; they do not have any interest in the classes and have traveled throughout the world to "be better cultured," as they say! These girls are obsessed with marrying someone who will make a "good match," someone their parents will find for them so they can spend the rest of their lives being Mrs. So-and-so. Most of them are Turkish.

The other group consists of the "loose" girls. They call them that because they are taking the Pill and go to bed with their boyfriends when they escape during the weekends. The Turks say that those kind will never get married because their boyfriends just want them in bed, and that when their boyfriends leave them nobody will ever be serious about the girls because they're already "spoiled goods." Of the women that share this house, the group that I like best are those who talk about politics and go to protests and support all the strikes, even though they don't know what the demonstrations are about. I love to spend the weekends conversing with them instead of going out—and when I do go out, they are the ones who take me to the most interesting parties where people dance, smoke, drink, and discuss the problems that Chile is having nowadays, and they try to propose solutions. At the parties I dance only if some boy asks me to dance, because you know that it would be horrible if I were to ask one of them. They would think us to be cheeky hussies. I don't know how to smoke, and when I tried to learn it made me cough so much that I nearly vomited in front of all the boys at my first party. Nor do I drink because I don't like the bitter taste of the red wines that they serve, and it also makes me terribly embarrassed to think that the older girls will find out that I never drank alcohol before. I also feel left out of the group when everyone has an opinion about politics and I don't know what to say because I don't understand what the "revolution of the proletariat" is about or what "capitalism," "bourgeoisie," or "yankee imperialism" means.

Marjorie, I would love it if you were able to attend this university and live with me in this boardinghouse because there are so many interesting people to meet and so very much to learn. I've only been here two months and I have learned more about people than in twelve years at the nuns' Catholic school.

Emma

May 2, 1969

Dear Emma,

Today I miss you more than ever because I love to tell you about things, most of all about curious ideas that pop into my head. For example: I have this strange, crazy friend who says that every time she bathes, the hot water cooks her private parts, and her servants have to bring her a special lotion of linden and valerian. Well, everybody knows what is happening because she always bathes at the same time of day and one sees agitated people bringing her fresh water. We observe all of this astonished, without saying a word. Or: my mother always says that we should follow Grandmother Helena's example, who would count to ten before speaking. I wanted to tell you of those oddities as well as, of course, about my father, who wears his winter boots throughout the summer. He is always worried that his straw hat will fly off and reads science fiction novels as if his life depended upon it. My mother is very kind and keeps the peace whenever one of the children screams while my father walks slowly along as if this beach were part of a story from *Lawrence of Arabia*. I must tell you how I entertain myself watching the couples at the beach cover themselves with towels, then squirm like cocoons as they touch each other on their private parts. My older sister says that is called sex and only older people are permitted to do it. But let them call it sex or whatever they like. I call it the cocoons in tattered towels.

The things that occur at the beach are very amusing, Emma. The most fascinating is, and I am not sure if you realized this yet, but there is a beach for the poor and another for the rich, as if the same sand could be divided. Sometimes I think that there ought to be cities for the rich and others for the poor. Don't you think so? Well, there is also a beach for the middle class, which means ladies married to public employees, among them physicians like my father. These people go to the beach early, obeying the schedules of their daily life. They eat lunch at noon when the siren sounds. Those very well off finally arrive at the beach at that time because they can stay up all night and act as if they were the living dead. And of course the poor housekeepers and their husbands come down to the beach at five o'clock in the afternoon when everyone at the resort is supposedly sleeping a *siesta* (although it is possible to see them moving under the sheets). Don't even imagine that they sit at the big beach, but instead the poor must go down to the small beach that doesn't have any canopies. They walk around completely naked! That beach is near fish stalls and piles of rotting fishheads. The women don't have swimsuits and I believe that they would be embarrassed to wear one. I see them lift their skirts and a little sun touches them on their dark, hairy legs. They laugh a lot. My grandmother Sonia is always asking why Christians laugh so much. I believe that it is because they were not the ones who killed Christ.

Well, Emma, all this about the beach is very interesting. My sister is beginning to make friends and she wants to go to the beach to dance. I am not interested in any of that, and prefer to be alone and read my books. I love my books. I like to pause before their covers, and at night I lie awake because of them and worry if they are sleeping well.

Marjorie

June 10, 1969

My dear Emma,

As I told you before, I've changed schools. My new school is called the Hebrew Institute of Santiago and it is at 1242 Macul Street, very near the Pedagógico, one of the most political places at the University of Chile where my father teaches. The students have very, very long hair—ideal, I imagine, for taking a nap—and wear exquisite clothes and smoke like chimneys. I like them because they are so delightful to watch. Perhaps someday I will marry a man with a beard. They say that to my sister, who dreams about them the same as I. You know that very well.

I like the school because it is nothing like that awful Union School. In the first place, here the professors are from Israel and are very young. Mamá says that they are socialists and almost all are part of a new movement called Hashomer Hatzair, one of the movements that founded the state of Israel. They wear shorts and they like to sing. I am extremely happy to be attending this school. The classes fascinate us. I study Chilean history, history of Israel, the Talmud, the Torah, and song. Can you believe that all these classes are in Hebrew? My grandmother Josefina, who I always tell you about, asks us why we are studying dead languages, but in my opinion Hebrew, with its marvelous alphabet, makes me happy. My father says that he had neither a Jewish nor a secular education. I'm not certain what "secular" means, but I like the word. It is tinged with a monumental elegance. Sometimes, my mother says that poverty is for the secular and I smile at her. I don't understand her, but I smile nonetheless.

Well, my beloved and adored Emma, I like knowing where I come from, understanding my origins and truly being able to answer when they ask me: What are you, Chilean or Jewish? I am sure that they don't ask you these things, but they always ask me and whenever important people visit our house, they say things like: "Of course, you're Jews." What do you think of all this, Emma? Life is complicated and I wonder if when we are older, will they ask us the same questions? What will our lives be like and where will we be? My mother always says that we Jews have to be ready to leave for places unknown, to live as if we had a suitcase packed and waiting. But then I wonder: what would we do with Papi's piano? Furthermore, all this about always being alert and on the defensive has been very beneficial to me, for I always know how to answer back.

Until later, Emma. When we are able to see each other, I hope they allow me to spend a few days at your house.

I love you,
Magi

✳

April 14, 1970

Dearest Emma,

The winter is beginning to create its enchantments. No one especially likes this season, but I think that it is a lesson about the beauty the future holds, like the Spring that lies dormant, deeply asleep, preparing itself for the sun and the light. There are things that I like about it, like eating the roasted chestnuts sold by the street vendors. I believe it is more the idea of the chestnut than real chestnuts that attracts me because my mother told me she and

my father used to make them in the fragile first moments of their
incipient love. But what I like most is to go to Carmencita's or
María's rooms. The nannies always live in the darkest rooms of
the house, in the most secluded rooms, in shamefully sordid corners. I feel sorry for them and ask them what they did when they
were young. Then they show me photographs of their mothers
about whom they know so little. The mothers they show me are
young and don't have many teeth. They also tell me of outings on
the rivers, of the Christmases when they had no gifts but instead
exchanged fruit, especially cherries, and of a recipe for Christmas
bread made with raisins to help the memory.

I spend a lot of time in their rooms. I listen to their radio soap
operas, mostly the one about the very pretty and scandalous Es-
meralda of the river—a baby girl abandoned in a silver basket, a
tale similar to the story of Moses. You know, my dear Emma, perhaps my family and I are part of these rear rooms. Someday I will
tell you how hard it is to be Jewish in a country that constantly
reminds you not only of what you are not, but also that you are
not as they, that you were the murderess of Christ, that they will
carry you off in the middle of the night to baptize you, that you
don't belong to fine families with long last names, and that you do
not possess vineyards. You yourself told me that in Mendoza you
heard a lunatic priest screaming against the Jews. But I assure
you that I didn't kill Christ. On the contrary, I would like to kiss
his wounded temple and, like Mary the Jewish mother, dampen
his forehead.

You know, Emma, the thing I like most about being in these
rear rooms is that I feel loved by them, by these nannies, in a way
that I don't know how to explain. I feel loved and embraced, cod-
dled and sheltered. I inhale that scent of oregano, of the rich
things of the earth. Sometimes we go to the garden and these
women know the names of all the flowers, even their last names!

I like to see them bury their hands in the dirt as if they had
surged from the earth, as if happiness were jasmine, orange blossoms, and a moment of peacefulness.

I especially like to draw near to them and hide my head in
their percale aprons scented with cilantro. When I am afraid, I al-

ways feel that their aprons will save me and protect me more than all other things that might give me refuge and the truest faith.

Magi

June 1970
La Serena, Chile

My dear friend Marjorie,

My final class of the day this afternoon, the Theory of History, seemed to last forever. Hegel's ideas that my classmates were discussing seemed distant, remote—I wanted to talk about today, about now, about Chile. I didn't know with whom I can share this overwhelming emotion that completely fills me. My classmates are all political militants and cannot understand a young nineteen-year-old woman who is just awakening to the fever of ideologies and changes being experienced in our country. I am embarrassed to open my mouth at our meetings, so I listen and think . . . think and dream.

All my disquiet began this morning when I listened to the presidential candidate Salvador Allende in the patio of the university. I am still floating on a cloud!!! You cannot imagine what it was like to see him in person, listen to his ideas, and shake his hand when he passed before the multitude of students. I had prepared a couple of things that I wanted to say when he walked in front of us, but as he drew nearer to where I was standing so many thoughts came to mind that I stood there frozen and mute—I could not even smile while he shook my hand and said, "I need your support." Can you believe, Marjorie, that great man, one who has tried to win the Chilean presidency in so many elections, who has traveled our country from north to south, came to our small university in an out-of-the-way city in the North, to give a speech and tell us that our vote matters, that our vote is necessary, that our vote can and should change the destiny of our country. But moreover, he is the only candidate who has come to speak to us about our responsibility in the political process and has told us, without promising us heaven or threatening us with hell: "I need your support." Marjorie, my friend, it is the first time in my life that an important politician has shaken my hand and looked at me as a person. I swear to you that I am never, ever going to forget this.

The speech given by Salvador Allende will also be etched in my memory for the rest of my life because he said that in order to leave behind underdevelopment and find our true destiny on the global stage, we have to educate our youth, liberate the working class, and nationalize our natural resources. Also, he spoke of the injustices that are committed in the countryside where it is not only the laborer who works for a beggarly wage, but also women and children work in the fields without earning a cent. He said that by means of Agrarian Reform, "the earth will belong to the one who works it" and the few landowners who own every inch of land in our country will have to relinquish their control, for good or for bad. In his speech he declared that the factories will also be in the hands of the people, the same people who will carry him to victory in September, because "a people united will never be defeated." All day those fighting words have resounded in my ears, those words that challenge the bourgeoisie and speak of the victory of the oppressed (whom my companions call "the proletariat"). Based on everything he said, I believe that if Allende wins there won't be any more poor people in Chile, if Allende wins everyone will have work and food.

Before he finished speaking, he attacked Yankee imperialism and he blamed it for launching a campaign inside Chile in an attempt to prevent the victory of the leftist alliance. I didn't understand that part very well because, with the little that I know about the United States, I don't believe that it would meddle in the internal affairs of another country. He also had accusations against what he called "CIA," which is, according to what I have heard from my classmates, an organization in the USA that is dedicated to secret investigations, that is to say to watch people like the policemen do. I don't understand anything of this either because if it is an organization of the government of the USA, one of the most powerful countries in the world, why would it be interested in a little country like Chile and in a presidential election that is like so many others that we have had throughout our history? Although I do not understand very well what was said about imperialism and that agency that is like the police, with the little information that I have I honestly do not like that country at all.

Allende's visit caused a tremendous commotion in La Serena and our campus because people on the right paid groups of students to stand in front of the university with signs painted with things like: "With Allende, Chile will be like Cuba," "Allende stop! Russia wants you," and "*NO* to Communism!" After his visit, all the students and professors who supported Allende went downtown to parade with signs. I, as always, following the advice of my friends, joined the march with a huge sign that said "We Will Triumph." I could barely hold up that immense piece of wood, and when the wind blew I was dragged wherever the sign went, from one side to another without any control, following the demonstrators who screamed like lunatics, repeating phrases Allende had used in his speech: "A people united will never be defeated . . . a people united will never be defeated!" When we arrived at the square in the center of town, those who are against Allende were still carrying their signs, and they began to scream at us: "Traitors!" and "You are selling out our country!" and "Are you Fidel's children!?" along with other things that I didn't understand. In the blink of an eye, the square became a battlefield where women were hitting each other with their purses and men were striking out with anything that they could find in the street. You know I am not very aggressive in those situations, and since I still had that enormous sign in my hands, I was hit by a lot of purses. The police arrived and they immediately sprayed us with water cannons and threw tear gas that made us cry uncontrollably. At that moment I decided to defend myself using the sign and I opened up a passage in the crowd. When I approached the edge of the crowd I threw down the wooden sign, and at that moment a policeman saw me and began to run after me. I was so afraid that he would catch me and take me away in the bus with the other "revolutionaries," and I would be detained. I ran like I used to run in the races held at school, I ran toward the corner of the square and upon turning the corner I ducked into a restaurant and headed straight for the bathroom. I waited for a long time, while I heard the noise of the bombs and the police cars, I waited until I could not stay in the restaurant anymore and I went out slowly into the street and, with my eyes watering from the gas, I walked until I arrived at my boardinghouse. As I arrived, the widow who ran the house was waiting to inform me that she had called Santiago in order to warn my father that I kept company with revolutionaries because, if I were suddenly assassinated, she didn't want to have to bear that tremendous responsibility. I do not know how that old goat keeps track of the "ladies" who live under her roof—she seems to know what we are doing every second. I also found out, after I arrived at the boardinghouse, that two of my housemates had been detained during the confrontation, and would have to wait in jail until their parents came for them and paid their fine. The two are from very well-known families and have money, so the fine will be dismissed—and the poor policemen who detained them will suffer when their superiors punish them for stopping girls who belong to the Chilean aristocracy. There are so many things that we need to change in our country!! I strongly feel that we are living in an historic moment in Chile now, and we young people are those who have the opportunity to see that the dreams of a great future become, for the first time, reality, not only in this country but throughout Latin America.

Don't forget, Marjorie, we will triumph.

Emma

❈

January 7, 1971

My dear Emma,

As I told you in the letter I sent you last week, I am anxiously awaiting the visit of my relatives from Viña del Mar. I am very timid and it frightens me to be among so many people. Also—and

I can only tell this to you—I often talk to myself. I sometimes
spend the entire day talking alone. You know, I have a small ball
of wool that my *nana* Delfina brought me from the country and I
spend the day with it playing in the backyard, near the acacia
trees because I like the scent. In addition, I like that spot because
it is the sunniest and most isolated part of the house. My nanny
likes to tease me and calls me an old witch, but my mother, whom
I have loved since I first saw and even until now I rarely argue
with, she tells me: "Talk to yourself, Magita, you go right ahead
and talk to yourself." And with that I pass the time talking alone
and I feel very happy doing it. When we return from our vacation
I will tell you about all the characters that I have created. I don't
like to pretend to be a professor when I can play at being a world
traveler, a navigator, a painter, or the explorer of the Orinoco.

Emma, on Sunday my mother got up at the crack of dawn
with Delfina and began to dust. All mothers have the mania of
dusting before guests arrive. My sister and I felt ourselves being
dusted and nobody paid us any attention. At about eleven o'clock,
when the sun was perfectly wonderful, so exquisite, they arrived
in a van because they all wouldn't fit in a car. There were about
twenty of them and they slowly got out of the van. The last to exit
was Aunt Lucha, the one who bathes the dead. She got out at the
end, directing the "traffic" of my relatives' arrival. They brought
borsch, that Russian-Jewish soup made from beets and they say it
can resuscitate the dead. They brought their famous gefilte fish,
made the Jewish way, and my great-grandmother Sonia hummed
the Ochichornia. You know Emma, these relatives seem to have
come from the important families of Russia who became exiles,
families that have come down in the world yet hold firmly to the
beliefs of the past. My family speaks Russian, Yiddish, and German. The truth is that they have difficulty with Spanish, and also
we like to be different. Not to make us feel better than others, but
because it is something beautiful to be from somewhere else, and
among ourselves nobody insults us and makes us feel very uncomfortable, nor does anyone say to us: "Oh, of course, you're Jewish . . ."

Well, my dear Emma, my relatives stayed until close to midnight. After eating, they took a nap—some of them slept on the floor. A fly crawled into my young uncle's ear. Everyone laughed because they were reminded of Uncle Deresunsky who scratched his ear all day while he read the Talmud. After our nap, we went back to eating: pastries and the indispensable chicken and avocado sandwiches. I envy people who are able to wear crosses and eat foods scrambled together . . . pork with cheese, milk mixed with meat; being kosher already implies a mountain of rules but, according to Uncle Isaak, it has to do with the protection of life. I love you and will protect you.

I will continue telling you things. With all that going on, I could not go out to the patio and talk to myself, and the worst thing is that the watermelon fell on my thumb. Aunt Lucha said that it was Francisca's curse because they didn't bring her with them from Viña. Well, I was left with a swollen thumb and an earache. They put olive oil and garlic on me. These homemade remedies horrify my father, but since he is the only man in our house Delfina, and sometimes Frida, give the orders.

Ciao, Emita, until later.

Marjorie

❋

February 23, 1971
Asunción, Paraguay

Marjorie my friend,

I am in Paraguay. As I told you when we saw each other in Santiago, I had saved some money and that, along with some financial help from my father who rewarded me for the excellent grades I earned at the university, let me put together enough to buy sufficient U.S. dollars for a trip by land to Argentina and Paraguay. With the new changes that are taking place in Chile, the millionaires are taking out their money and depositing it in Swiss banks or in other countries, and everyone is buying dollars wherever they can for the going rate on the black market. One cannot travel, as you already found out, without showing a visa from the country you're visiting or a bank permit in order to buy dollars. My father purchased my permit with the highest limit that he could and he gave me just enough for my modest trip. I took what he gave me and with that and my savings, I left in search of dollars on the black market. My friend Jenny, who is my traveling companion and a classmate from the university, found a contact in one of the shanties of the slums in the hills of Coquimbo. By the time we returned home to Santiago for Christmas vacation in December, we had already purchased enough dollars to take a trip by land through Paraguay to Argentina, and then fly back from Buenos Aires directly to Santiago.

We left by bus at dawn on January 9 and, like I have done so many times, we crossed the beautiful Andes mountain range en route to Mendoza. Bearing that brutal, burning heat of Mendoza in January, it took us five hours more to arrive in San Rafael where we visited María Rosa and the whole Italian-Argentine and Italian-Spanish "mafia" (family!!). After eating sausages, ham, grilled meats, and all the pastas made exclusively from original recipes of the Pulvirenti family, we continued on our way to Rosario, where we stayed in a convent with my Aunt Coca, who is a Carmelite nun. It was an interesting experience because I still want to know the secrets of the nuns in my family. I spent many hours talking with my aunt and she finally confirmed what my mother had told me: she became a nun because she had fallen in love with a Jew, and neither he nor she wished to convert. So, as I understand it, she wanted to punish herself and him also—although he apparently did not suffer very much because he married another Catholic who didn't have any problem with becoming Jewish. I spent the whole time in Rosario visiting friends of my aunt. At first they looked strangely at me until my aunt told me to stop wearing tight-fitting skirts and bell-bottom pants. All the clothes that I had brought were like that—the latest styles—so my aunt bought me a blouse with typical Paraguayan embroidery and a skirt that covers my knees, an outfit that makes me look like a perfect idiot. The visits are all to houses of lonely old women or to families of fanatical Catholic parents who always have about ten children because they don't believe in family planning or birth control pills. One of the most interesting visits was to the church in the town square where one of the priests looked at my aunt as if he were in love with her. I believe that there is something between them.

Because of the macho rules of the Catholic Church, she must treat the priest as her superior, because nuns are like the priests' servants, and he orders her around as if she were domestic help — but she is brighter and better educated than he. During all the time I stayed with her, a day didn't go by that we didn't visit Father José, and on many of the visits I was left waiting for her outside the church.

After that familial parenthesis in our trip, Jenny and I continued on the road to Paraguay, where we had one of the worst experiences that a person could have in a foreign country. We spent a few days visiting my friend David, a volunteer with the "Passing" Corps (that's what we call Peace Corps!!), in the forest. After that visit where we had neither drinkable water nor bathrooms nor electricity, we decided to spend the last few days of our trip "as God would wish" — in comfort — so we booked a room in the best hotel in Asunción! On Thursday night we went to downtown Asunción to buy blue jeans imported from the USA, because you know that nothing from outside is imported to Chile now. We bought two pair each. The saleswoman made a mistake and gave me one of the pair in a size too large, so we had to return to the store the following day to exchange them. Upon arriving at the store I looked for the same saleswoman, who recognized me immediately and then handed me five pair of pants, pushed me into a changing room, and quickly locked the door behind me. I was scared when I found myself locked in, but then I thought that perhaps it was a Paraguayan custom to lock the doors when the stores were very full, and I calmed down. I took my time and when I was finished I banged on the door. When nobody opened the door I began to scream, and suddenly the door was violently yanked open and I found myself face-to-face with a group of armed soldiers who were pointing machine guns at me. I was completely terrified — I had never had a weapon aimed at me and I had never seen uniformed men act that way. Two of them grabbed me by my arms, pulled them behind me and handcuffed me. I began to cry and asked what I had done and why they were treating me like this. They wouldn't respond to my questions and the only thing they did was repeat: "You know very well the shit that you pulled!" After handcuffing me they took me away, pushing the end of the machine gun barrel into my back until we reached the main cashier's station of the store, where my friend Jenny was also handcuffed and surrounded by soldiers. They opened our billfolds and took out our passports and all the money that we had left. A man identified as "the manager" said yes, we were the criminals, and after signing some papers and giving them to the soldiers, they began to push us along again and they told us "no talking among yourselves . . . and now, to jail." We went out to the street and they put us in a large van, then they took us to a detention center that was a few blocks from the store. There they put us in a dark room where the only thing you could make out [was] small windows with black bars, and where there were drunk people vomiting, half-naked women, and other people handcuffed like us. We spent a while there without being able to speak to each other, crying the whole time. Then a soldier called from the door "Jenny Rojas!" My friend got up from the floor and, without even looking at me, went with the uniformed man. What seemed like a century passed, and when Jenny returned her eyes were very red and her hair undone, and the same soldier said: "Emma Sepúlveda." I stood up, speechless with terror and looked desperately at Jenny, hoping that her eyes would tell me something, anything that could warn me of the danger, of what they had done to her. Jenny did not look at me and I left, followed by the soldier, not knowing where he was taking me or of what I had been accused. We entered a hot room where there was a table full of papers and a chair. At the table were seated three men in uniform. They made me sit in the chair facing the table and the young man who had taken me into the room stood behind me. One of the older men began to speak, and he told me that my friend Jenny had confessed that we were members of a counterfeiting chain that was trafficking in phony dollars. He said if I confessed also, they would release us immediately. I realized at that moment why we had been detained, but I was even more shocked about knowing that perhaps my friend Jenny was involved in trafficking counterfeit dollars. I started to cry without knowing what to say, and when I lowered my head in order to cover my face with my hands, the soldier standing behind me grabbed my hair and jerked my head backward. A terrible pain shot through my head and neck, and I told them, desperate, that I didn't know anything and please don't hurt me. They answered by ordering the young man to slap me on the face and pull my hair as hard as he could against the back of the chair. Marjorie, you cannot imagine the awful pain that I felt nor, at the same time, the helplessness of being unable to say or do anything that could transform those monsters into human beings who would listen to me. They continually repeated that everything would be easier if I confessed that I was part of an organization of international traffickers. But in spite of my terror I kept insisting that we were innocent, and finally I screamed that Jenny would never do something like that because her father was a captain in the Chilean army. There was a sudden silence and the young man let go of my hair. One of the three interrogators stood up and asked me the name of Jenny's father. I answered him, crying: "Juan Carlos Rojas." The same officer ordered the young man who had pulled my hair against the chair to look for Jenny. When Jenny entered the interrogation room, she looked at me for the first time since this ordeal had begun, calmly, and stopped by my side. The officer asked her: "What does your father do and what is his name?" Jenny confirmed the information that I had given him. The old man gave orders that they remove the handcuffs and take us to his office. They escorted us, this time like human beings, to the office of the older officer. The office was dark, had old furniture and a strong scent of cigars. The old man, now extremely civil, asked Jenny where she had purchased the dollars and if we knew anyone in Asunción. Jenny, very self-possessed, told him in detail and also mentioned something that surprised me. She said that Mr. Palacios, whom we had met the previous night while we listened to harp music in the restaurant of the hotel, was a close friend of her family in Chile. The officer was impressed, picked up the phone and called the hotel. After a few minutes, Mr. Palacios answered the telephone, and the officer explained the situation and, without our knowing what Mr. Palacios had said at the other end of the line, we listened to the old man say: "They'll be waiting for you here, Mr. Palacios."

While we were waiting for Mr. Palacios to arrive, they offered us something to eat and drink, but we told them no because we were still terrified. The Paraguayan gentleman arrived and Jenny greeted him with a kiss on the face. The officer apologized to him for causing him this trouble and said: "If these young ladies had told me that they were innocent and that they knew respectable people in our country, we would not have interrogated them." Mr. Palacios asked how we could "arrange this matter" so that the papers signed by the manager of the store would not be kept on file, and the military [officer] said, "I believe that about a hundred dollars would take care of those papers." Mr. Palacios took out a wallet full of dollars, although that is not the national currency, and gave the officer a hundred-dollar bill and two twenties. The soldier then ripped up the papers that he had on the table, gave us only our passports, and told us that he was sorry, but the rest of the money was counterfeit. When we asked for the Paraguayan money that we had with us, he responded that surely the people in the store had lost it because he had received nothing more than our passports and the dollars. We went out onto the street, free, with this Mr. Palacios that Jenny had only met the previous night when she discovered that he is the well-known owner of a television and radio chain in Paraguay. When we arrived at the hotel, I went directly to our room, but Jenny stayed to talk with the famous Mr. Palacios in the terrace of the hotel. Jenny is twenty-five years old, blond with stunning blue eyes, and without a doubt the old man liked her since he met her last night. I remained alone in the room for a while, thinking about how we would be able to leave Asunción and get to Buenos Aires without a cent in our pockets . . . then Jenny returned and said that the Paraguayan millionaire would send us from Asunción to Buenos Aires in an airplane and that, after spending a few days in Buenos Aires in a hotel near the obelisque—all expenses paid—we would return to

Chile. All this would be done by using companies that were his clients in Paraguay and Argentina. Apparently the old man not only liked Jenny, but also had said that he felt terribly embarrassed by the behavior of his countrymen, the military.

We are still in the expensive hotel of Asunción, paid for by Mr. Palacios, and Jenny has already told him that she has a fiancé in Chile and that they are getting married in a few months (all lies!!). Every night we push a piece of furniture against the door because Jenny says that the old man might come in and rape us because he is paying our bills. Thank goodness that tomorrow we are going to Buenos Aires and from there to Santiago. Marjorie, you can't tell any of this to your family because we have to take this secret to our deathbed with us . . . and if my father were to find out, he would send me to an early grave. I hope this serves as a lesson to you and please never, ever buy dollars on the black market.

Until I return,
Emma

March 1, 1971

My dear Emma,

I have many things to tell you since my last letter. Well, summer has ended and my mother stopped allowing me to wear white pants and let my hair grow like the other girls instead of having it cut in a pageboy style. I like to dress all in white, as if I were transparent, and those are the clothes that I wear when no one is watching me and I am able to devote myself to my imaginary games. I still play at being a single mother, although I do not exactly understand what that means, but it has the hint of the forbidden and the grown-ups turn red when I tell them of these games. But that is not what I wanted to tell you. What I wanted to tell you is that I now have two temporary sisters, Silvia and Tamara Broder. They have come to live at my house for a few months while their parents are getting settled. They are the daughters of a first cousin of my grandfather. They don't speak a word of Spanish, and they laugh and say, "Ya, ya, ya," and I say "Yes, yes, yes." I know very little about them, or about their house and lives in Prague. My mother tells me that it is very sad to talk about the war and I sometimes see her sobbing, wandering like a sleepwalker through the rooms. Grandmother Helena, my great-grandmother, the only one who speaks German, also weeps when she converses with them in Czech. The servants say that Jews are diabolical, full of secrets, and that they were put in ovens as if they were beef to be roasted. When I say that to my mother she becomes silent and rigid, and she says to me: ". . . no more, no more." Meanwhile, I feel important with my foreign cousins. Suddenly, and perhaps for the first time, I understand what it is to be from another place and never to belong to any one place in particular.

Yesterday we carried out our traditional visit to the dressmaker, who talks with pins in her mouth. She made us the blue uniform that ought to be exactly the same as yours, but ours [is] distinguished by having a star of David on the jacket. I wear it proudly, although sometimes during contests with other schools they spit on us.

I love you in a quixotic way, as would say Miss Marta Alvarado, our history prof.

Magi

✳

December 1971

Dear, dear Emma,

I write "dear" twice because today I discovered that the Spaniards kiss twice, a kiss on each cheek. They are true kisses, not ones in the air as the women from "high society" (as my mother calls them) do here. It makes me tired, Emma, that everything is divided based upon the neighborhood where one lives and the schools you attend. Clearly, to say "Hebrew school" already implies that everybody knows that you are a little Jewish girl, a poor thing with a big nose who wears castoffs. I am looking for a

[handwritten margin note: often refers to people + class]

country where people are accepted as they are, where nobody sees color or neighborhood or address. I think that perhaps North America might be like that because I have seen in American movies that servants eat with their employers, and there are no bars on the windows of their houses—there are no noises or other interruptions. Is that what the other America is like?

Have you noticed those people who dress their maids in green aprons and put a bell on the table to summon them? Because of that my father says it is time we had a socialist government. We like Allende. His brother has visited our house many times, and he and my father argue about the role of medicine and health care. They say that this is the true problem of our country: having good health care for everyone. Once I visited the Our Savior Hospital that is quite near your house. Do you remember, Emma? I was tremendously shocked when I entered because there were flies and dogs, and the patients were wandering around, unable to find the busy doctors. Once I found some bloodstained cotton. Can you imagine those unfortunate sick people, using rotten bandages?

Notice that I am writing you this letter while you are in Mendoza because I worry about this country of ours. Of course, who doesn't love their homeland, their earth, their trees? But I feel that we will leave. My father is very enthusiastic about going to Israel. He is not a fanatical Jew, but I believe that he is in love with socialism. In my school they don't like Allende, and people believe that he will rob them of their jewels and their houses. I understand some of that because there are many classmates whose parents were uprooted from Czechoslovakia, Hungary, and Russia, and I see the fear cross their faces.

We are not afraid, but I am terrified of leaving here. I am beginning to write my first poems and I read them to my teacher, Mr. Alvarez. He caresses my hair and tells me, "Keep this up, dear child, and you will be Chile's second Gabriela." But who loved Gabriela? They accused her of being a thief, they tossed her out of schools, they called her a repugnant lesbian. Could that be my fate or is it the fate of all poets? All this talk of socialism has made me careless. I cannot tolerate seeing the maids with their green aprons and making gestures of reverence. I cannot tolerate hearing the people here say: "My God, doesn't he have an awful face like an Indian!" What does it mean to have the face of an Indian, of a Jew, or of a servant?

I don't know how you are feeling, but I am concerned that we are neither free nor different. In vain we all try to be equal and yet be different than others, but it is pleasant to be alike, to fight for the same things and, as my father says, to have the right to health, to the same toys, and to be able to study piano if one wishes.

So, Emma, what do we do? When will we see each other? I am going to write you from El Quisco because we leave in a few days. And you, I'm sure that you have already gone with your cousins to Mendoza. I hope that the nun behaves herself.

Love you,
Magi

❋

February 1972

My dear Emma,

I am writing you from Quisco again. As it happened, my Aunt Lucha invited us to spend a few days in Viña del Mar. Of all my aunts, she is the one that I love the most, although she is constantly telling everyone about her operations, her aches and pains, her bunions, and the red pills that she has prescribed herself. I enjoy talking with her about Gabriela Mistral, about the Bible, and many other things that make me happy. She says that I am going to be a writer. The truth is that I already am, and I spend my time making notes and spying on certain people whom I love intensely. I have magical notebooks and pencils.

My Aunt Lucha has four children, all wonderful young men. The truth is that I like one of them and it doesn't scare me that he is my cousin because, as you know, my papá and mamá are cousins. I like Marcos, who was a paratrooper in Israel and has affairs with their maids. (Now they call them housekeepers, but they are treated as badly as before!) That is what he talks to me about while the women sip rich vermouth and the men drink martinis in odd glasses that are shaped like a woman's body. Well, as I was telling you, at night I dream about Marcos and I wake up blushing, as if someone could discover my dreams. They say that sex is scary, but I love thinking that somebody could kiss me all night and that I would take his breath away, like I saw in the movie *Gone with the Wind*.

Well, my beloved Emma, the other day I had to go play with my rich cousins—girls who are fairly ugly and in their family they all have their noses fixed. But what worries me, almost obsessively, is that my cousins like to give us used clothing, and make a big ceremony of giving us dresses like nuns would wear, old and wrinkled, and odd things with ruffles. My mother, whom everyone calls "Frida the Refined," accepts the gifts—but I don't like those clothes because they are not offered with love, and they tell me things like "it is because your poor father is only employed by a university."

But how they would love to have a papá like mine, one who is wise and even plays piano at midnight. This ceremony of the used clothes irks me, and I believe I will put them in their place one day. I noticed that in their house there are no books, only spare parts for automobiles, and I do not like that at all. It is a suffocating home, without books and without words. I tell this to my Aunt Lucha while she corrects my spelling, and she tells me that it would be better if we talked about the Bible. Aunt Lucha is right. Being poor is a serious thing, and my father is always telling us not to worry because we are intellectuals. But I want to know: what does it mean for one to be an intellectual . . . in order to suffer such headaches? Not all intellectuals are poor and broken. These phrases . . . I have listened to them my whole life, Emma, and I cannot tolerate them. I want to be a hairdresser or perhaps the owner of a bazaar. I also want to tell you that what I love most about my Aunt Lucha is that she affirms that survival is in itself already miraculous, but to survive as Jews . . .

Magi

✳

December 20, 1972

Dear Emma,

We have packed all our suitcases for the long vacation that awaits us on the Chilean coast. We will enjoy three months filled with water, sunshine, long walks—just thinking about it makes me feel deeply and deliciously happy, as happens to you during your days in the countryside. Emma, my mother packs numerous cans of preserves that she then gives to the people in the area. We already know them because we have gone to their houses, and I believe I understand a little of what it means to live near the sea—that life of great hardship and overwhelming happiness . . . returning home with fresh fish, their scales the colors of pearl and gold. I understand the deceptiveness of winter and the candor of summer. I believe that someday I will live next to the sea so I can dream of its dreams.

Our activities are very simple. What may seem to many a great bore is for us delicious—like having velvet days all to myself in order to enjoy, to be, to write in my blue notebook long, leafy poems of love and sadness, of liberty. I like the word "liberty" because it is melodious.

During the mornings, we rise and hurry to the water. I do not dream at night about being a queen or a princess. I find it more interesting at night to dream about being a slave and, like the Egyptian Jews, to think of my escape. But anyway, we go to the beach. My mother takes her knitting, my father his science fiction novels imported from Buenos Aires, wearing his shoes laced very tightly and a coat because my father sees the world in reverse: he bundles himself up in the summer and strips down in the winter— he votes for losers and goes out for walks in the darkness. All those things have ceased being strange to us. That is what my papá does, Emma my love, dear Emma. We are a family of eccentrics, but I prefer it and I consider it much more normal to speak to the dead than to talk to plaster statues.

Very good. relationship w/ family

After the beach we return home warmed through and through, with an exquisite flush, a marvelous fatigue. Awaiting us are salads with tomatoes and lots of onions, because without onions there is no accompaniment for main dish nor appetizer. But I remember what the poetry of Don Pablo Neruda says: "Ode to the tomato — That it is the tomato which is true sovereign at all times." Do you think, dear Emma, that without a tomato there is no salad?

Sometimes my grandmother Josefina visits, whom we love madly. As ever, she has the habit of not finding things as good as they were in her house. For example, she is always saying that this thing or the other did not please her as much as it could have. We are always in expectation, wondering: what will she find fault with now?

After our lunch, which is long, we take a nap if my father is not home. Husbands only come to the coast on the weekends and so they're called "summer bachelors." I go to my mother's room. It does not look out on the sea but instead onto the street. I like to be near her because while she sleeps I dream that it is my turn to look after her, to shelter her, to protect her from the air currents. I like to know that in the afternoon I will hear other noises like the people strolling by, the lovers, the drunkards—and the sea, so crazy, so ferocious, safeguarding me in the night.

After our nap we drink tea, because although ours is a poor and languid country here at the end of the world, we have the audacity to think that we are part of the British empire and we crazily drink tea in the late afternoon, a civilized tea, while we talk about the servants and worry about knowing who has the face of an Indian or who remained in Santiago because he didn't have money to take a vacation.

Dear Emma, what I like best after eating my bread and avocado (and when Mamá is in a good mood and not worrying so much about our ancestors) is when we satisfy ourselves with delicious cured ham. I like to go out and walk, to feel that air so sweet and at times so filled with moisture on my nape. I love feeling the night arrive to us, very dense, the nighttime next to the sea, the beautiful night, the golden night, where I will dream that I was a slave and I now am free or I will dream that I am an Araucanian princess and happy to be so.

AMIGAS

Emma, such is life here: three months of tomatoes, onions, fried fish, and walks along the beach. Some days my mother says that I will attempt in vain to return to this time, but I know I will remember these days as the most wildly happy moments of my life. Tell me of your days, of your summers and of your life abroad. Is Mendoza abroad? If so, you are already an important woman and, of course, more than being an intellectual, you are a worldly one.

Marjorie

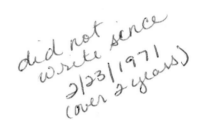

May 1973
Santiago, Chile

did not since write 2/23/1971 (over 2 years)

My unforgettable Marjorie,

I returned from Venezuela a couple of weeks ago. I definitely could not live there. There is no place in the universe like Chile. I hope with all my heart we never have to leave the mountains and unending, open skies that surround us.

The news flash that I have to tell you is that one of my socialist classmates, Alfonso, has finally noticed me after all these years. He is supermilitant and I admire him devotedly. Almost everything I know about politics I learned from him by silently following him during the meetings, and listening to his speeches and his comments in class. Marjorie, he's the perfect man for me in my dreams, but not in reality. If I were to fall in love with a man like that, it would destroy me. I feel it is terrible that our generation is only thinking about the socialist revolution . . . it seems we want to set aside everything else in our lives. We do not want a love that requires a commitment, we don't want to have a single, special person in our lives, and we don't want romance. The only thing we love is politics, and we reject anything that might interrupt our struggle or interfere with our ideals.

I want to aid the revolution, but I also want to have a human connection with other people. I long to experience a permanent relationship with one man, and I don't want to deny myself a future with children because they say that I must, instead, be dedicated to upholding the socialist ideals of my country. Could this be lack of commitment?

Last week I went to a party with my classmates, and Alfonso was there. He danced with me, and my body seemed to become weightless in his arms while he held me around the waist. There were moments when I felt as if my feet didn't touch the ground . . . I was floating. I could have stayed in his arms forever, but our realities are much too different. Alfonso is worldly and experienced, I am a young lady who was raised within the oppressive walls of a Catholic school, a *señorita* from the upper class. Alfonso is known as a Don Juan, and all my girlfriends have been in love with him at one time or another. I would only be another of his conquests, nothing more.

At the party, Alfonso asked me again not to marry Michael. It's not that Alfonso is in love with me, the problem is he can't accept the idea that I would marry a gringo. Doing that would be committing an act of treason against our political cause, I would be accepting capitalism, imperialist intervention in Latin America, and everything else we do not want from that country. What does all this have to do with my marrying an American? After all, I would never go live in the USA.

Alfonso knows that I adore flowers (although that makes me a sweetly romantic woman and that is unacceptable in these times). At the party tonight I told him jokingly that even if he were to fill the porch of my house with flowers, it would not prevent me from getting married the next week. You are not going to believe this, but at three o'clock in the morning he called me and told me to open the front door because he had left a surprise for me. When I opened the door, I discovered that our entranceway was full of flowers, of all colors and types, piled in huge heaps from one end of the room to the other. It was a sight to see! The next day, I found out that Alfonso and some other classmates had stolen all the flowers that the military units, in order to commemorate the

Battle of Iquique, had placed beside the statue of Arturo Prat in downtown Santiago.

I am struggling to find the strength deep inside of me . . . part of me wants to toss everything aside, cancel my wedding, and allow myself to be swept away by Alfonso's madness. But there are two things that stop me. First, I believe I am in love with Michael and it is already too late to turn back. The second thing is that I have always been terribly afraid of someday falling in love with a Don Juan like Alfonso. So I have decided to go on, forget my doubts, and get married.

Do you think that everyone has doubts before getting married?

How do we know if this is true love, the one that lasts forever?

Marjorie, dear heart, everything is becoming so complicated as the years pass. Call me soon. I am a little lost without your advice this time.

Lots of hugs,
Emma

✳

July 1973 ⟨2 months pass⟩
Santiago, Chile

Marjorie, my friend:

While Chile continues on its dangerous path towards chaos, my family has suffered a terrible tragedy that changed all of our lives forever. A week ago my mother had a dream in which she saw my brother dead in the arms of his friend. You know our relatives are very superstitious—they believe in the powers of spirits and in premonitions—and since the night Mamá had the dream I was unable to concentrate on my teaching practicum that was to prepare me for our professors' classroom visits. But on Friday her dream became a horrible, living nightmare. At eleven o'clock that night, I received a phone call from a friend of my brother Hugo, who advised us that there had been an accident with his truck and that Hugo was in the emergency room. When I went into my mother's room to tell her, she completely lost control and began to scream that my brother was dead. I tried to calm her and explained, no, that he was alive and we should leave immediately to see him in the hospital. We left the house running and caught a taxi, but as we were getting in the cab I realized that my brother's friend had not given me the name of the hospital, so I asked the driver to take us to Nuñoa Hospital, which was near our house. When we arrived and asked about my brother, we were told that nobody with that name had arrived that night, and that seriously injured accident victims went to Central Hospital because it was larger. We took another taxi to Central Hospital. We were told by the receptionists that there was no information at all about my brother, and they explained that when cases arrived that were extreme emergencies, they didn't register the patient immediately. When they saw our desperation, they allowed me to enter the wards and look at the patients in the rooms so I could identify my brother. After going through a gigantic metal door and entering a narrow room, I came face-to-face with the stretchers on which men and women were crying, moaning, and begging that they stop the bleeding, that they give them a sedative or that somebody help them to breathe. The odors, the screams, and the images of white cloth bathed in red filled me with an uncontrollable anguish. I walked between the stretchers searching, looking at faces, listening to wailing, trying to see the big, dark eyes of my brother Hugo, his eyes that would speak to me and tell me that everything was all right. I went through rooms and corridors, between the sick and wounded, doctors and nurses, but I didn't find him. I went out to the waiting room and rejoined my mother, and told her that we would need to continue our search until we found my brother. It was already three o'clock in the morning when we left Central Hospital. In another taxi, we arrived to the emergency room of the Saviour Hospital and everything repeated itself—I again wandered rooms full of people slowly dying, women and men screaming with pain, and wounded bodies that twisted with bloodstained wails. My brother was not among the victims in the hospitals, and that encouraged us—we thought that the accident could not have been serious and, by this time of the morning, Hugo surely was waiting calmly for us at home. When we returned home it was already six a.m., and the sun was beginning to show itself from behind the Andes mountains that surround Santiago. As we were closing the door, I heard the telephone ringing and ran to answer it. The voice of one of Hugo's friends sounded desperately from the other end, and he told me that we needed to leave quickly because my brother was in Nuñoa Hospital—the first place we had gone!—and his condition was serious. We left the house again, running once more like crazy women. We arrived at the hospital and discovered that my father had already spoken with the doctors and knew the details of the accident. Apparently, Hugo and a group of young people were riding in the bed of his friend's truck while it was being driven at a high speed and, while they were turning a corner, those in the back flew out of the truck. Hugo tried to protect his girlfriend and had hit his head on the curb when he landed. Now he was unconscious and the doctors did not know if he would ever recover. We entered his room and saw him lying on a small white stretcher, his eyes half-closed and his mouth twisted in pain. My mother hugged him and cried, and held him in her arms for a long time, until finally my father and I separated her from his stretcher. During those final hours no one could do anything for my brother, we could only wait and pray to God that this would not be the last time that we would see him alive.

His condition was unchanged during the next few days. The strikes in the hospitals and the poor medical service made it impossible for my brother to receive the necessary care or the intravenous serum he needed in order to survive his terrible accident. On Thursday he regained consciousness and spoke to us for the first time. He asked my mother not to cry, and he asked my father and me to take him out of the hospital because he didn't want to die alone between the cold walls of that white room. Although his voice broke, he made an enormous effort not to cry, and as he said those last words, tears rolled down his face . . . he looked at me with his dark eyes filled with sweetness, and he said once more: "You can't let me die—you love me too much to let me die." We held hands tightly and I promised him that I would never let him die.

On Friday at 5:00 a.m. my father came into my room to tell me that my brother had died. I asked him not to tell my mother until we took her to the hospital so that they could give her a sedative. Between the two of us we helped her to the hospital, and convinced her that she was going to see my brother before they took him to the operating room. When we arrived at the door of the hospital, my mother pulled free of my arm and ran up the stairs to the room where my brother had been. Some minutes later I heard a scream that seemed to have risen from the bowels of the earth, a harrowing and eternal scream, that resounded on the white metallic walls of the old hospital. Nobody could calm her until they managed to give her an injection that took the shine from her eyes and changed the youthful tenderness of her face into a sad and aged mask. Since that morning my mother has never been the woman she was before. Losing her second son the same way she had lost her first is something that she will never overcome as long as she lives. She had challenged fate—because everyone said that after our first brother had died, she should not have given the same name to their second son. José Hugo was born already marked by destiny, and cheated death until he was seventeen years old.

The following day, they carried his body in a blue coffin. It was as if he had known that death would be waiting for him around that corner because, some weeks earlier, he told me that when he died I was to do everything possible to prevent them from putting him in a black coffin. The service was at the chapel of Our Savior Preparatory School. Throughout the day, friends and family wept, overcome by their tremendous sadness, as they said good-bye to somebody who had been taken before his time. All his classmates stood alongside his coffin for most of the day.

The mass took place on Sunday morning. My mother remained beside the coffin without taking her eyes off my brother's face and with her hands clenching the edge of the wooden box. I decided not to look at my dead brother because I wanted to keep him with me, his eyes and smile full of life, sealed within my heart forever. When my father and the rest of our friends and family approached the box to close it, it seemed my mother could not open her hands to let loose, for the last time, of the blue box that contained the lifeless body of Hugo. When she finally opened her hands and the box was closed, there echoed through the church the last lonely scream of my unfortunate mother.

After the funeral, we walked slowly along the paths of the General Cemetery of Santiago and I believe that, for the first time, I began to realize how life is one of the most fragile things that we will encounter in our journey. Everything the nuns taught me in school has now become meaningless because I believe that there is not life after death.

I hope you come to Chile this summer so that we can walk on the beach, and you can help me search for peace and resignation after the death of my dear brother.

Best wishes,
Emma

❇

October 23, 1973
Santiago, Chile

5 mos total

3 months pass

Dear friend,

After the military coup of September 11, things have become difficult for all of our people. Along with the workers, peasants, political activists, and other groups in the country, we young university students will pay a very high price for the support we gave President Salvador Allende.

Last week in *El Mercurio* there was an announcement that asked all students in the final year of their program to report to their universities so that they could be processed to receive their degrees at the end of the year. When I read the notice I was frightened — I thought they were luring us back to the university so they could identify those of us who had eluded arrest the day of the coup, and we would be detained and interrogated. My mother insisted that I had done nothing against "the democratic values of Chile," and that I had the right to receive my degree after five long years of study. My father, of course, talked about the good political connections that he had in General Pinochet's new regime, and said he could speak directly with the president of the University of Chile and they would allow me to return to my studies without a problem. After listening to the advice of my family and all my friends who knew of my situation, I decided to go to the university on the date indicated in the newspaper.

When I got off of the bus, I saw that the street in front of the university was packed with students and that all the ironwork gates were closed. I approached the multitude without recognizing anyone until from a street corner someone screamed "Emma!" My classmates Mónica and Corina were among the students waiting for access to the campus. I went and stood with them, and as I approached them I felt a strong sensation of coldness and distance between myself and my friends. They greeted me soberly, and asked if my husband, Michael, was happy with the results of the CIA's plan in Chile. I didn't know what to tell them, and when I tried to ask them why they had such an idea, they told me that we shouldn't talk too much because nobody knew who in the crowd was a member of the Chilean secret service. I also asked them why they hadn't called me, and they answered that nobody could rely on privacy while on the telephone now. Marjorie, I cannot express what I felt during those moments, seeing my country torn, ripped to pieces, and my dear friends now separated due to fear and distrust. Nobody knew who was who and nobody spoke, nobody dared to look at or recognize a face that might connect them to the past, or may condemn them to an uncertain future filled with interrogations. All were separated and disconnected, one from another, but closely united through the shock and torture of our fear.

We waited under those conditions until, through the loudspeaker, a soldier's voice told us to line up in front of the main door. The line extended more than a block and turned the corner. We were near the beginning. When my turn arrived I was petrified with terror—all the soldiers were pointing their machine guns at the students and shouting orders at them. The girl who entered before me suffered the humiliation of having her trouser legs cut off while the soldiers told her: "From now on, women in our country will dress like women!" Seeing what they had done to her overwhelmed me with fear. As I passed through the main entrance, two soldiers grabbed me, one on each arm, and they held me so that other soldiers could search my body. I was wearing a short skirt and a blouse. The soldiers felt me all over in order to determine if I had weapons or anything else hidden on my body. Then, as one of them held me stiffly upright by twisting my arms behind me, the other one rubbed his hands between my legs and down the neckline of my blouse. I felt violated, insulted, and reviled at the deepest level that a human being could feel, but I couldn't protest because the soldiers kept their guns aimed at me . . . then those who had searched me pushed me from one side to another and made certain that there was not a single centimeter of my body that didn't bear the marks of their hands. After the search, they took away my identification card and my wallet, and then two soldiers led me to a room where other students were waiting. Another group of soldiers was posted in front of the room to ensure that nobody spoke or communicated with anyone else in any way. We were held there for almost an hour, until the room was filled with enough students and the process could begin. A soldier gave a speech, saying that we were fortunate to be alive considering we had abandoned the obligations of the "true university student" because we had meddled in politics. He told us: "From now on you will come here only during the exact hours of class and afterward will go home, no one will speak in the patios or in the hallways, nobody will go to the dining hall, and absolutely nobody, nobody, will ever talk about politics within these walls." He added that before we left the room, each one of us had to sign a document and, if we didn't comply with these orders, we would be punished "to the full extent of the law under the military government." Then they passed around a sheet of paper and told us if we wanted to finish our programs and receive our degrees in December, we would sign it; but if we didn't accept the conditions, we should not sign it. Nobody said anything. I received a copy of the form and read it, my hands wet with perspiration. It began "I _____ (name of the student)," followed by a blank line for our national identification card number, and ending with a declaration that we had not directly participated in the govern- ment of Salvador Allende and that we would never support a left- ist government in the future. Then there was a list of promises re- ferring to the nonpolitical behavior that we should maintain if we were accepted again by the institution and permitted to finish our studies.

Marjorie, you will never be able to imagine what I felt at that moment, and I assure you that all the other students felt the same way. The alternatives were to acknowledge that we had supported Allende and be detained immediately, or lie and know that we would always be loyal to our cause but we now needed to do what we could to survive this nightmare. I was heartsick . . . I thought about my classmates who had already disappeared, about the bod- ies that had covered the streets of our tormented country, and I knew I had to live so I could tell their stories and never stop fight- ing for the right to be free. I signed the paper and raised my hand, as we had been told to do when we were finished, and I waited until a soldier came to retrieve the paper and grab me by the arm to take me out of the room. Outside, two other soldiers almost dragged me by the arms to the entrance, where they gave me my documents and my wallet. As I walked again down Macul Street, that street I have known for so many years, so familiar in my life, I felt the tears roll furiously down my cheeks and I realized that my life would never be as it had been before.

The following day, I again joined the multitude of students who waited for the soldiers' announcement of who could re-enter the university, but my only two classmates who had come the first day were not among the crowd of students. For four days we waited outside the closed doors of our university, without receiv- ing any response from the soldiers, and without being able to talk among ourselves because we did not know who was with the se- cret service and who was a student. On Friday, finally, through a loudspeaker, a soldier began to read the list of students who had "clean records" and could resume their programs. My name and those of my classmates were not on the list. After he read the would not be readmitted to the university.

Marjorie, I am afraid to remain in Chile now that I realize that my name is on some secret government list for reasons that I do not know. I have a terrible sensation of uncertainty about my future—and the future of all my generation that had hoped to live the dream of a free country and have ended up facing a desperate nightmare.

I'll write again soon.

Emma

✳

December 1973

My dearest Emma,

I do not know how to begin this letter . . . for every beginning there is also an end. This is an ending, a very sad farewell, filled with anxiety. This will be the final night we sleep in our house on Simón Bolívar Street, and tomorrow the last morning I will awaken and see the Andes mountain range and tell them "Good morning, Chile, I love you . . . here I am again with you." Emma, we are leaving for the United States, and I have spent days sobbing quietly because I do not want to leave my house, my garden, or my trees that today are full of cherries. I do not want to leave forever with only the suitcase I carry, nor do I wish to leave my poems that are kept in a coffer, filled with orange blossoms, that my grandmother brought from Córdoba. For the first time I have a complete and exact awareness that nothing is ours, and that perhaps my grandmother and my mother were right: that we Jews should always be prepared to flee, with our bags always packed, ready for an escape.

I wonder what it will be like to sleep in other cities and not in this one, in my dear Santiago, where my parents were also adolescents, where they loved each other madly in the plazas and swore their eternal love that is everyone's love.

It is here that I have my history, as inconsequential and distant as it may be, but I have absolute confidence that it is mine. From this patio I articulated my first words, the alphabet became harmonized with my hands and my breath. Who shall I be in those other lands? How can I resign myself to the perversely remote idea of being a foreigner for all time, or an exotic guest, always inopportune?

My head is a wreath of flames, rotating . . . darkness falls and yet things are becoming clearer, as in the movie about Scarlett that I liked so much, especially when she said, "Tomorrow is another day." What will my days in Georgia be like? How will I begin to reconcile myself to poems written from afar? Will someone be able to read verses that I write in a strange language?

Throughout this night the murmur of everything beloved—the rivers, the breeze, the names of the stars—has accompanied me as if it wished to remain with me as I return to the foreign words and icy perspiration that truncate my speech. I am afraid . . . and accompanied by the certainty that those lonely days will draw near when everyone will ask me over and over to repeat my name and I, perhaps, will forget its origin.

Magi

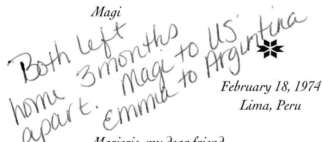

✳

February 18, 1974
Lima, Peru

Marjorie, my dear friend,

I left Chile on January 4 with a profound sadness in my heart. I feel as if my body has crossed the Andes mountains but my soul remains on Chilean soil, trapped among my family and my lifelong friends. Nobody and nothing had the right to take from us our immense happiness, our freedom, and our dream of a better future for our people.

Before getting on the bus that would carry me and Michael to Argentina, I bent down and touched the earth with my hand, the land that was under my feet, as a silent farewell to my roots and my people. My family and close friends came to say good-bye. We cried, as we always cry in my family at weddings, funerals, and partings. As the bus began to pull away, I turned my head and looked back. It was as if my memory took a final photograph, one that I will carry with me forever. I saw the desolate face of my mother who was losing her third child, the face of my father as he made one last effort to smile and accept the impossible, and the hands of my friends as they waved, hoping to give me strength in these final moments of our deep sorrow.

Marjorie, leaving Chile was to leave behind a piece of my being, a part of my life that I will never replace but, most of all, I've left my soul, my free spirit that had wished to build a future with my people upon soil scented with tears and work, children and dreams.

On the evening of the fourth, we arrived at my grandparents' house in Argentina. As you know, my grandfather Silvestre died a few years ago and my grandmother Concepción is not in very good health now. Many of my cousins and uncles were waiting for the bus from Mendoza, and when we arrived at the house there was an enormous celebration with music and food, as the Italians in my family always do. We talked about my decision to go to the United States and of how difficult my new life would be in a land far from the customs and intense love that anchor our culture and family. For them, it was as if I were leaving for another world, going to a distant and unknown life, a life that, according to them, could not make me happy. My grandmother told me that grandfather Silvestre always used to say that the most painful thing in this world is the life of an immigrant, because you will never be part of your new country but you are unable to return to the life you left behind. My grandmother said, from that moment on, I would be a woman without a homeland of any kind.

I spent a few days visiting what seemed to be an endless number of relatives and celebrating an eternal farewell in the Italian-Argentine style — and, after having said good-bye again, we left in a bus destined for Paraguay. During the next several days, I traveled through places I had visited with Jenny. I'll tell you, nothing has changed, except that the poor have become poorer, and there

68   are more soldiers in the streets with machine guns, men who have the faces of inquisitors. The children continue begging in the streets, the young girls are still looking for clients during the hot nights in Asunción, and poverty invades every corner in the cities and towns of that country.

After Paraguay, we enjoyed the phenomenal madness of the Brazilian carnival. I spent several days traveling through the exotic, exuberant landscapes of the Amazon and dancing samba in Rio de Janeiro. Few people in the world have the rhythm or the emotional and physical abandon as do the Brazilians when they dance during their carnival in February.

Now I am in Peru visiting ruins and towns hidden in the highlands. Since the trip will be long and we haven't much money, we have stayed in cheap hotels and boardinghouses . . . not only are they dirty and uncomfortable but they also attract young people who are waiting to buy good drugs at reasonable prices here in Peru. I had never imagined that there could exist this underworld built around the consumption and sale of drugs in our countries. My years in the nuns' school protected me and distanced me from many realities, and because of that I am now twenty-three years old and have great difficulty understanding people my own age whose lives are so different than ours. Last week at two in the morning, while we slept in a humble room of a small hotel called "The Spring" located near Cuzco's main plaza, the police arrived and all the guests were made to go to the patio and stand in the rain. The police were looking for drugs, and so they put us out on the patio and searched all our baggage and even the clothes we were sleeping in that night. After finding the culprits—two girls and two young men from Holland—they allowed us to return to our rooms. A young man who spoke a little Spanish explained that they had purchased marijuana on the street and hadn't known that in Peru it was illegal because in Holland it was not against the law. I couldn't sleep the rest of the night thinking of the fate awaiting those young people. They would spend months in a horribly dehumanizing jail, awaiting a trial during which they would already be considered guilty, without access to what they would consider a basic right—an impartial defense—because in our countries you are guilty until proven innocent.

AMIGAS

Today I saw Machu Picchu for the first time. The trip to the ruins was an odyssey. I took a train from Cuzco to a town near the ruins, and from there I had the brilliant idea of experiencing the culture as the Indians do. I decided to ride in a truck loaded with potatoes that also carried passengers on top of the cargo for a very small fee. The Indians who were waiting for the truck told me that the trip was difficult but not extremely dangerous, and that was enough to convince me that if they could do it then I, too, had the ability to journey the same way. When the truck arrived, the people went crazy trying to climb up as quickly as possible because the truck would stop for only a few minutes and then the door closed, and the ones left behind had to remain behind, and nobody could request a reimbursement of the fare. When I put a leg on the edge of the truckbed, I had the good fortune of having a fat Indian woman behind me who, with Herculean strength, shoved me on my butt and threw me, head first, into the middle of the potatoes and the laps of the other Indian women. With the weight of my backpack it was hard for me to stop sliding down the pile of potatoes. The truck began to climb the mountain and, with all the strength I could muster, I grabbed the dresses and the legs of everyone around me until I stopped. I was only settled for a few minutes when the road began to curve and the potatoes shifted under my feet, causing me to fall over again. The same occurred with each curve, with each rise in the road, and with each push from another woman who was also trying to maintain herself upright on the floor of potatoes. I believe I could have tolerated the trip if it were only the potatoes on the floor between our legs, but when the people who were standing up began to get sick and vomit on the others, I lost my patience. I not only lost my composure but also the strength to keep my breakfast in my stomach, and I began to vomit on the potatoes, Indian women, and their children who stayed quiet, strapped on the backs of their mothers. The women battled to recover their poise and clean the collective vomit, which nearly covered them completely, off of their clothes. In our desperation we all helped each other. And when the truck arrived to the top of the mountain and stopped, somebody opened the upper part of the door and we began to get out like crushed livestock, hurried by the blows and screams of the driver, who threatened to leave although we hadn't gotten off of the truck. So it was, the truck left and many of us ended up on the ground wet with vomit and bruised by the blows we had received while on the road. When I had managed to compose myself with the help of my fellow passengers, I realized that these women traveled daily under those conditions in order to sell their products in the neighboring town. Our women live an amazingly hard life and never complain, and furthermore accept their fate with admirable stoicism. Marjorie, I do not know how I am going to tolerate this trip. It is physically difficult—I have never had a pack on my back for more than an hour . . . much less wearing the same pair of pants for weeks without washing them. I can't bear to continue sleeping in hotels full of fleas where I am afraid to get undressed to go to bed, and where I am not able to bathe or wash my hair day after day. Could this be how the hippies in the United States live now?

Well, friend of my heart, I will write to you in a couple of weeks when I am in a better mood. I received the letter you sent to me care of the United States consulate in Lima. I will continue going to the consulates in the capital cities to receive my correspondence, so don't stop writing me.

Greetings to your family.

Emma

※

March 1974
Guatemala City, Guatemala

Dear Marjorie:

I continue my travels through Latin America, and I am discovering little by little what the loss of democracy has done to this continent. Almost all the countries I have visited have military governments and their people live in a constant state of panic. We will all remember the 1970s as the most terrible, shameful period of Latin American politics. It pains me to see the streets awash in poverty; it grieves me to witness how the division between the haves and have-nots is so marked, and the way it irreconcilably separates our people.

Guatemala is a country both colorful and sad, seemingly peaceful yet inundated with weapons. The indigenous population does not have the same rights as the mestizos or the whites—they are treated worse than animals, without a shred of dignity nor any respect whatsoever. On the buses the Indian women, although burdened by their children on their backs, have to give up their seats to any white person that gets on the bus. The whites do not ask them for their seats but instead brutally push them aside, so that they will make way for those who "deserve" the privileged places.

My journey across South America has been a slow farewell to that which was my life, my culture, and my history. I know that it will be difficult to return along this path someday and re-encounter this past that is left unfinished because of my departure into the exile. Every time I enter a different country, I feel the same sensation of having crossed the threshold of a space that I know intimately, but is yet strangely foreign. I believe that the military presence in these lands causes me to feel separated from my identity and my past. . . . The dictatorships have taken them from me.

I have been in Guatemala for a month and I haven't been able to obtain permission to cross through Mexico into the United States. I had the same problem in almost every country, because Chileans are personae non grata outside of Chile at this time. We have been accused of seeking political exile in order to escape a military regime, and in each country there have been difficulties in obtaining a tourist visa. When I first arrived to Guatemala a month ago, I went to the Mexican consulate in Guatemala City and, as a condition of acceptance of my visa application, I had to complete a document confirming that I had not supported Allende's government, I wasn't a member of the Communist Party, and that I would not request refuge in Mexico. I have returned every two days hoping they've made a decision, but I'm always told the same thing: they have not yet decided and I would need to come back later. I have explained to them that I already have an immigration visa from the United States, but the Mexican government will not permit entry of any person from Chile at this time. We are a "marked" people, considered undesirables by most of the continent, although we have done no harm.

Two days ago I also went to the Chilean embassy to request help. I had hoped that a letter from someone there would help me get a visa for Mexico, but they refused to help me. At the embassy I was told that they could not support any Chilean citizen traveling abroad for reasons of national security, because they did not know if that person had escaped from Chile after having committed a political crime and was wanted by the government. I had never heard of anything so ridiculous . . . because if *they* did not have that information or a list of wanted criminals, who would have it? It's a shame you can't get help from your own embassy when you need it. Will we always be victims of our civil war even when we are not in our country?

The only thing I can do now is fly directly to Los Angeles from Guatemala City without stopping in Mexico. This will be my final night in this country and my last night among my people. Tomorrow I will fly across the border that separates my familiar, beloved past from an uncertain and unknown future. I am dreadfully afraid of leaving everything I love so much and entering a world that I have always rejected.

Marjorie, I am deeply saddened, and I am beginning to doubt whether I can live and truly be happy in the land of Uncle Sam.

Love,
Emma

Marjorie and her mother, Frida Agosín, during a sunny but cold winter in Washington, D.C., where she was born. She is six months old.

*Marjorie, her sister Cynthia, and school friends on
Marjorie's birthday in Santiago, 1960.*

Marjorie's class at the Hebrew Institute in Santiago, 1972. Many of her classmates left the country during Pinochet's regime; others disappeared.

Marjorie with her former nanny, Delfina Nahuenhual, who raised her. The photo was taken in Quisco, near the place where Emma and Marjorie met. Delfina also took care of Emma many summers. Delfina is a direct descendant of the Araucanian Indians. She is still alive and takes care of Marjorie's grandmother in Viña del Mar.

Marjorie and her husband, John Wiggins, in Athens, Georgia, 1977.

Marjorie, Emma, and Chilean writer Pia Barros in Honolulu, Hawaii, at a writers' conference, 1987.

Marjorie and her children, Joseph and Sonia, in Wellesley, Massachusetts, 1998.

Marjorie's beloved grandparents, Joseph Halpern and Josefina Halpern, in St. Mark's Square, early 1960s.

Emma, age 14, 1964.

Emma, age 20, during her second year in college, La Serena, Chile, 1970.

Emma's wedding day,
August 16, 1986.

Emma, her husband, John, and son,
Jonathan, 1994.

Mailer sent to the voters during Emma's campaign for the Nevada state senate in 1994.

April 17, 1974
Los Angeles, California, United States

Dear Marjorie,

Yesterday Michael and I arrived in Los Angeles. This world is so very different from mine! Since the moment the airplane landed, I have been miserable knowing that I am among people who don't understand me and treat me as if I were from another planet. Some friends were waiting for us in the airport and they immediately took us to a Mexican restaurant so that I would feel welcome. It was a great surprise for me because I had never eaten Mexican food in my entire life and, moreover, I was not even permitted to enter that country some weeks ago. I arrive here and they all believe that I am Mexican as soon as they set eyes on me.

We drove through some of the neighborhoods in Los Angeles so I could see how people live here on the other side of the border, here in the North. I wanted to walk, breathe the air, and look at the people up close, and perhaps talk with someone who lived there in the eastern part of the city, but they told me that nobody, absolutely nobody, walks through those neighborhoods because if you do, they will kill you. What kind of civilization is this where the people can only go through the neighborhoods in cars? And how do the people who live there survive? How do their children go to school? I hope that Los Angeles is not representative of the rest of the USA, because I don't know if I can live among high-speed freeways and people deaf to the pleas of their neighbors or the cries of the children.

I consider it a city made of iron and inhumanity, where everything moves at extraordinary speeds, and nobody says anything and nobody listens to each other. In the restaurant where we ate all the workers were Latinos, from the ones who washed the dishes to those who served the food. The food was very strange. Although the menu was in Spanish, I didn't recognize anything on it. There were things called "tacos," which for us means a part of a shoe, and something else called "burritos," and I also did not understand what that meant. I couldn't imagine that we would eat food made from donkey meat, so between the limited Spanish spoken by my friends and the explanation of the waitress, I found out that Mexican food is totally different from the cuisines of South American countries.

I feel totally lost these days. I cannot understand anything people say to me, and I am desperate because I am not able to make myself understood. It is as if I am wrapped in an absence where my body is present but my mind escapes with my thoughts. The sounds of the English language ring in my ears like monotonous noises, senseless and oppressive. When I try to say something in English, people look at me as if I were stupid and they don't pay attention to me. It seems that they don't like people from other countries.

Marjorie, I would have never imagined how different this country could be to the fantasy that we see on television and in the movies. We always thought that everyone living here was a millionaire, and that the streets were clean and everything was white. What I have found is totally different. In my entire life, I have never seen such a combination of races, languages, and neighborhoods. Nor had I ever dreamed of seeing such poverty. Poverty is sadder here because of the tremendous contrast between those who have so much and those who don't have anything.

Tomorrow we go to Nevada, to the city of Reno, where we will live permanently. The only thing that I know about that city is that people get married and divorced there in the blink of an eye. I think Reno will be like the towns in the cowboy movies, a city filled with gunmen, bars, and casinos.

I will try to phone you now that we are in the same country again. Don't write me until I send you my permanent address in Reno. I am happy knowing that we now will be close to each other and we will see each other more often.

Love,
Emma

April 1974
Georgia

Dearest Emma, my beloved friend,

It has been a few months since we arrived in the United States, to an empty, frozen house. Papa's immense piano looks so alone in the middle of a living room that is without furniture and guests. Yesterday I watched my mother spend hours at the dining table, which is also empty. She was listless and melancholy, and said that this table would be lovely if it were filled with people. It is so odd to have left our country. It is as if we are suspended in midair. We are glued to the television, but we never see any news about Chile. I have realized that they do not even know where our country is.

I have drawn small maps of Latin America, and I color Chile very blue. It is so thin, like a marvelous, delicate strand of spaghetti. I am consoled by my drawings of our homeland, which now seems so far away, as if we've never lived there.

Tell me, Emma . . . have you thought about what a homeland is? Certainly it has nothing to do with a national anthem, although there are times I long to hear, to say, to say aloud "My homeland" and "Viva Chile."

I feel very lonely, Emma. People make fun of me because I cannot pronounce some English words. A teacher told my mother that I ought to attend a "special" class. My mother thought it was an English course, but I realized that it was a class for children who can't learn anything, children who forget everything. But all I want to do is remember, and I wander through the house seeking the scent of hyacinth, honeysuckle, and lilies. It fills me with sadness not to tread the soil of my country; I feel I cannot catch my breath, I have lost my sense of time, I am off balance. I left Chile, and it is as if I have put on two mismatched shoes, and now that I am far away, I notice that the shoe that stands in North America is black and the one that remains in Chile is blue.

I love you,
Marjorie

June 7, 1974
Reno, Nevada

Dear Marjorie,

My first month in Reno has been an experience I will never forget. This city is in the middle of the desert, and everything looks white and sterile. There [are] practically no dark-skinned people and almost nobody speaks Spanish. We are living in a tiny apartment where I feel trapped, and I am afraid to look out the window when I hear a noise. All this is so different from the world I left behind in Chile. In almost all the apartments of our small complex live people who work in the casinos both night and day. Some arrive home drunk in the morning, and they get into fights that terminate with a visit by the police; and at night there is always some woman who hits her partner and they end up arguing, shouting insults that I don't understand and physically attacking each other, which troubles me.

Two weeks ago I went to the city employment service. They made me fill out papers and answer all types of questions, and afterward some guy who knew almost three sentences in Spanish interviewed me and tried to explain things to me, but I didn't understand him. After an hour they called me and I returned with Michael so that he could translate, and I was told that I could get a position as a maid in a hotel or a dishwasher in a restaurant. I got a knot in my throat, but I didn't cry. I realized that I would have a long, hard road ahead of me if I wanted to find my place in this country. As we left the office and walked in silence under the terrible afternoon sun, we decided to follow the advice of our friend Bill, who had suggested that I look for work in one of the

Mexican restaurants in Reno. At least there I could communicate with other people while I washed dishes or cleaned floors. I was lucky, and at the first place we went I found work as a "hostess," the woman that seats the people who come to eat. They gave me the position because I look like I'm from Mexico. They're paying me a dollar an hour.

The first day I arrived at work, I wrote several phrases in English on the palm of my hand: Good evening; How many people in your group?; Follow me; This is your table. I arrived early because I had to dress in typical Mexican clothes, with my hair full of ribbons, and my mouth and cheeks painted red as a tomato. When I finished dressing and looked in the mirror, I was so embarrassed that I almost ran out of the restaurant and returned to my apartment. But I knew that although this job made me look ridiculous, it was better than other work I could be doing.

Since that first day, I have seated hundreds of people and I have handed out hundreds of menus. I do not understand a single word they say to me, and I walk miles and miles, hour after hour, wearing those long, wide skirts and two hundred multicolored ribbons in my hair, smiling, smiling, always smiling, so that nobody will realize that I neither speak nor understand even one syllable of English—and they all think that I am a young woman who was brought in especially from Mexico in order to give an authentic flavor to the restaurant!

Many of the people who work here in the restaurant are in this country illegally. They come across the border hidden in the trunks of cars, under seats, or squeezed between the cargo of trucks carrying produce from Central America. The majority come without their families and are saving money in order to pay another "coyote" to bring their wives and children to this "promised land." All of them live with the constant, palpable fear of the *"migra,"* that is, the Immigration Service. A couple of days ago I experienced the terror of the *"migra."* It was eleven-thirty, and while customers were being seated for lunch, someone in the kitchen shouted in a desperate voice, *"La migra!"* In minutes the whole kitchen was emptied, and the employees ran like crazy into the street. The restaurant was thrown into chaos because nobody was serving food, and the customers were growing impatient because they had to return to work at one o'clock. The owner called together the remaining employees and we managed to prepare the tacos, enchiladas, and burritos. I felt like an idiot wearing that long dress and a ton of ribbons in my hair, preparing food, frying and boiling, and sweating like an animal. I could not read the words of the food orders because they were in English, so I assure you that nobody ate what they ordered for lunch. But at the same time I will never forget the words that I learned that day: chicken . . . beef . . . beans!!

Marjorie, you were right when you told me in your letters that life in this country was extremely difficult for the poor immigrant. I do not know how much I am going to be able to tolerate [it]!! I have not applied for a driver's license, so I walk everywhere. In this city there is no adequate public transportation, so to buy food I have to walk miles under a grueling sun and carry the bags home. There is no washing machine in the apartment, so I wash our clothes in the bathtub or walk to the laundromat with enormous bags filled with the sheets and towels that I could not wash by hand. My life has changed so radically in only a few months. Now I am aware of the privileged life that I led with my family. The maid used to do everything, and I could devote myself to being one of the "young misses" of the house, without responsibility for any of the domestic chores. Now, for the first time in my life, I have to live in a miserable apartment, I have work that I detest, and I do not even have enough skill to cook an egg. On top of all this, I am in a country that I don't understand nor understands me.

Every night before I fall asleep under the stars of Uncle Sam's country, I remember the words of your letters and I understand you much more now than before.

Write to me.

Love,
Emma

Dear, dear Emma,

Here we are in this America in the North, the America about which my grandparents dreamed but could not enter because there were few visas granted to poor Jews after the war. But that made no difference to them! They just arrived a little farther away, in Buenos Aires, while those who were more fearless went to Valparaiso. Many say that they lost their way and so ended up on the Atlantic coast near Buenos Aires. Did you know that my grandmother was born there in a Jewish neighborhood of merchants and traveling salespeople? Then, when she was three years old, they crossed the Andes mountain range by mule and there she remained, eternally, as a daughter of Chile, although during moments of anger, she would ask me if I knew what it meant to be a foreigner and then would say, "Well, when all is said and done, I am Argentine." My only response was a smile.

My dear Emma, I have discovered many feelings within me, and I do not know what will occur as our days now elapse with abysmal slowness. Suddenly we have been left with an emptiness inside of us, and my mother dedicates herself to staring at the only painting hanging on an otherwise bare wall. My father's colleague brought us some plastic chairs and with those we furnished the living room of the house. I miss Simón Bolívar 4926 so very much. It was a curious house in that, from the outside, it seemed small, unpretentious, but all one had to do was enter it in order to feel yourself inside the most fragrant forest, in a beautiful happiness, facing the timbers, and in the distance you could hear my father playing Chopin's nocturnes, while the orange trees could be glimpsed through the windows. I never thought about how much I would miss the exquisite dimensions of that place, certain pieces of furniture where my grandmother Helena had prayed in silence, the flurry of my mother's soft steps as she preoccupied herself with the stove, briskly fanning so that the flames wouldn't die down and, sometimes, her hands would seem a wreath of orange blossoms over tenuous fires.

Losing one's homeland is to lose one's voice. It is being and not being. It is to invent yourself in one language and then to be constantly inventing yourself in another for everyone else. At times I have felt that they forced me to invent a Chile that I never had, to be the ambassador of nostalgias that I have never felt, to pretend to love a country that was not ours. Emma, thus is our life outside of our house. Will I, someday, belong to this country?

Everything has seemed strange to us from the moment we arrived. The quiet city, the empty Sundays without balloons. Nobody strolls about in America. The people are taciturn and rarely laugh. I have been struck by how people are divided, one group living separately from another. For example, the rich and the poor, the whites and the blacks. Do not forget that we are in the South and I very much enjoy going to the countryside, which in fact is quite near the city, and I like to see the blacks in their chairs, balancing in their hammocks, twisting about, enjoying the light, the air, the happiness, time, and the present. They are the only ones, Emma, who seem to enjoy the Georgia afternoons, filled with the ethereal scent of magnolias that you cannot forget. Emma, we watch them from our automobile because it is our only form of diversion. To go out and see the world from the outside, anchored always to our nostalgia, to our anger, to the vicissitudes of forgetfulness. It is a country of loneliness and solitude. Nobody exits their cars to speak with strangers. Nobody argues. This is very different to what we experienced in Israel, where we spoke with everyone and they had ten answers to each question.

I find it difficult to sleep, and I wish to know what will become of us or when we will return to Chile. When my mother sees us troubled or uncomfortable with our new identity, she always tells us that this journey is temporary and that we will return to Chile very soon, to Chepi's house, and that we will accompany my mother to the festivals where all remember us, love us, and recognize us. Here, Emma, nobody knows about us. No one loves us and I am certain that nobody will ever love us. What is it to be a foreigner, Emma? Is it to be recognized through certain expressions or certain codes that have nothing to do with either our inner being or who we are at the moment? What does it mean to be from a place where everyone calls you by your name, where all embrace and recognize you, where you don't have to explain anything to anyone? This afternoon I closed myself in a closet together with a flying squirrel I found. I wanted to go back and surprise my grandparents in their gloomy bathrooms, but then I shivered. Where could I go? Whom could I call during these nights of pain and sadness?

Tomorrow is our first day of school, and I know that nobody will recognize me and I will have to invent my name many times so that, perhaps, somebody might hear me, might listen to me, and pause to be with me like before. I will put on my green coat for protection from all my fears. There is only one thing that makes me happy here: there is Coca-Cola everywhere!

Marjorie

❋

September 7, 1974

Dear Emma,

I went to my first day of school and quickly returned home. It was a terrifying experience. Everyone arrived by car and chewed gum in the parking lot. Then they went to classes through very cold, very dark passageways, and they closed their frayed belongings in lockers. Then we went to one class after the other, changing classrooms. I did not understand a single word. Neither the British English taught in Union High School nor our private lessons with Mrs. Berty had prepared me for this. I remember, Emma, that although it was September, I was very cold and put on my green wool coat. I always wear certain clothes and carry certain belongings, as if through them I could bring myself good luck and the refuge of love. But I then saw them laughing at my coat of wool, at my life, at everything contained within that coat: like the hands of my grandmother who had woven its fabric or the woman who had patiently spun the thread. Some boys, especially one of them named Charlie (it seems that all of the boys here are called Charlie), began to laugh uncontrollably at me, as if he had seen an apparition, as if it were the strangest thing in the world. Then I thought about the diary of Anne Frank, and I no longer felt alone among all those strangers. It was, perhaps, the first time that I felt deeply Jewish and punished for not being as the others.

But I had no choice. I had recently arrived to this odd land where I did not belong. Even the names of the flowers discharged the strange air of a people not my own. Who was I among those solitudes? Not even the trees were familiar to me but, yes, the *Diary of Anne Frank*, a faithful and silent companion of all the dreams I have found and lost, and those I have yet to find. Afterward, I thought about that fragment of the diary in which she herself says that people who do not live in confinement do not understand being surprised before a blue sky or the marvelous colors of morning, or birds that laugh and call greetings. I thought that, in spite of everything, I was alive, and I could awaken and feel my own breath, my own steps on that and other dawns, and I remained still for several seconds contemplating my own respiration that seemed to me the only possibility of contact with another voice that was not my own.

Hours passed until I decided to walk home alone. My little brother came to find me when I was halfway there. My mother was beside herself because of her sorrow, and I suddenly felt that we were full of light and that we were not alone, that despair should not be part of our lives, and we finally headed for home whistling.

On the following morning, I felt the same misery and pain, but little by little I felt the presence of invisible things or the sound of an unknown bird, the breeze over the moss, the clicking of the heels of my grandmother's shoes, and so I went and made myself strong among the expressions and the bleakness. I was not alone. I kept reading the *Diary of Anne Frank*; I kissed my mother's hands, as she did mine. I played with my brother. That was my life and nothing more, although we were so, so far from home.

Magi

AMIGAS

✳

Dear Marjorie,

A few weeks ago I began to study at the university again. The owner of the Mexican restaurant, after seeing me cry every night as I left work and knowing that I was miserable because I was working from sunrise to sunset without being able to save enough money to pay for tuition, called me into his office and offered his help. He and his wife gave me a complete scholarship, a special one, that pays my tuition, books, and health insurance. The only thing that I must do is continue working for them and earn good grades in my classes.

I have not yet learned a lot of English, only what I have taught myself, alone, so it is difficult to follow the lectures in class and take notes about what my professors are saying.

I changed my major from history to literature because what they offer in the universities here, as you know, is very different than in our country. Here they study a little of everything, but they are experts in nothing. I believe that with the little I know about literature, and having studied Latin American history for five years, someday I will be able to teach once I complete a degree.

The classes are incredible. I had to take a course in English for foreign students. It is something new in this university, so there are only ten students in the class. Three are from Latin America and the rest are from Europe and Asia. The professor doesn't know how to speak any language other than English, and no one understands what she is trying to tell us. The class is a disaster!! The students must give oral presentations, and we all memorize words and read as best we can what we have copied from books and dictionaries without understanding exactly what is being said . . . and, of course, the rest of the class does not understand either. When a Chinese woman spoke of their typical food and said that they ate everything with "lice," I learned the word thinking that it was the English word for *arroz*, and I repeated it many times and practiced saying it until somebody told me that it was the plural of "louse."

The university here is very easy in comparison to ours in Chile. Here, if you study you receive an "A" and end of story. As you know, in Chile everything was totally different because the grade of "A" was reserved for God and for those who knew more than the professors!

You cannot imagine how much I have to push myself in order to fulfill all of my responsibilities during the day. I earn extra money for food and rent through the "work study" program at the university. I arrive very early in the morning and, because I do not speak English, they have me do work that nobody else wants to do, like spending hours pressing the button of the photocopy machine and preparing coffee for the secretaries and the professors. After that job, I run to my classes and from there to the restaurant. Now I work as a waitress and I serve food to the customers and take their orders. I still confuse many of the words, but it is difficult to get very lost using the same, familiar vocabulary: enchiladas, tacos, and burritos. The most difficult task is carrying the hot metal plates on my arms. I burn myself almost every day . . . but I don't tell anyone so that they won't send me back to being a hostess. After I leave the restaurant at one o'clock in the morning, I go home in my small car that I still cannot drive well. They gave me a driver's license thinking that I was doing things wrong because I didn't understand what they were asking me to do, not because I really didn't know how to do it, so I am still not able to parallel park or shift into third gear without stalling the car. I arrive at the apartment and begin to study and, after a few hours' sleep, I begin the same routine again the following day. If this is the land of opportunity, I wonder what the other developed countries are like?

It is difficult and painful, this life of being poor and ignorant. I feel like a true illiterate in this country. I work like an animal to buy food and rent a miserable place in which to live. I never have a cent left over to buy an extra book or any of the other things

that in Chile I would have easily obtained. I do not know if I made
the best decision by coming to this country, leaving behind my life
as a privileged young lady to begin one as a poor unhappy immigrant unable to earn my keep or learn a new language well
enough to change my future. Sometimes I think that I should
leave all this and return to Chile, my homeland, the place where
people accepted me and I had all kinds of opportunities. I do not
know if I have what it takes to triumph in this country. In a few
months, without being able to control what was happening to me,
I went from being a woman considered white in Chile to a brown-
skinned immigrant, from an educated person to an ignorant idiot,
and from being privileged to being exploited. How did it happen?
Merely by crossing the border between one continent and another.

Phone me when you have time and a little extra money. Don't
forget the time difference, because the last time you called you got
me out of bed on a Saturday at four in the morning!

Best wishes,
Emma

✳

January 1976
Santiago, Chile

Dear Marjorie,

As I told you over the phone in December, my father sent me
the airfare to return to Chile. I needed to come back and see all
that I had left behind, and rethink my decision to live in the USA,
to be an immigrant for the rest of my life. I had to see both this
world and the other from different perspectives, and compare
them carefully.

More than two years have passed since that dark Tuesday, the
eleventh of September, that day when our souls were so deeply
wounded. This country is now dormant because of the fear. Nobody wants to speak of those who have disappeared, of the people

who are in prisons, of the ones who have been tortured, or of the exiles. Nobody speaks, nobody dreams. No one utters a single syllable in order to defend their human rights and the dignity of the country. All are encased in a terrible, impenetrable shell of terror.

My family is trying to convince me that the bullets fired from the rifles and machine guns at night don't kill people, they are only shooting into the air, they are firing warnings so that nobody goes out into the streets after curfew. My mother denies that in this country innocent people are killed every day. But the worst thing of all is that my mother, like all the rest, refuses to believe what she sees because of her fear. She is afraid to see the truth and to suffer the pain of our national tragedy. The streets are filled with soldiers and policemen. These same men that were our friends, our godfathers, our allies in town, are today our enemies. It is they who aim their weapons at you and follow you with their eyes and the barrels of their rifles through the streets, and even they themselves who interrogate you and torture you so that you will tell them what they want to hear. Because of this, people walk through the streets under the weight of their anguish, not knowing if the next bullet is meant for them, or if somebody will drag them away to be interrogated in some secret location in the city.

I have been unable to sleep these last few days. On Monday while I walked down the hazy street, amid the enormous lunch hour crowd, I saw a boy run out of a shoe store pursued by clerks who were yelling and gesturing. From somewhere in the crowd, shots were fired directly into the back of the young man, who fell facedown onto the sidewalk. I screamed like I had gone crazy until an old woman grabbed me by my arm and told me that I should be quiet because it was dangerous to scream in order to defend a crime. I controlled myself as best I could, and I obediently wrapped myself in the collective silence of the multitude that continued walking alongside the body that they had begun to cover with sheets of newspaper. I passed beside the dead boy and saw he was wearing new shoes that still had the price sticker on the sole, there was the evidence of his criminal career and the violation he had committed, for which he had been punished. The woman kept walking beside me and asked me where I was from. I responded that I was Chilean but that I now lived outside of the country. She took my arm so it would appear that we were friends, and she told me in a very soft voice, "Miss, we are in a state of war in this country, and criminals are punished at the scene of the crime, and the man who fired is a member of the secret service. They protect us from the criminals now." I gently let go of her arm and walked quickly, so quickly, and then, without realizing it, I began to run, and I ran until I arrived at a red light that made me stop suddenly, and I recovered my composure and caught my breath. I raised my hand and hailed a taxi. I told the taxi driver that I was late and so he had to drive as fast as he could, almost flying, to Suecia Street, to my mother's house. During the entire ride, I thought about the murdered youth and the old woman marked by the abominable indifference of defeat, who had chillingly described the new order established in our country.

I have not been able to visit my classmates from the university—all the phone calls I have made have been in vain because their telephones are disconnected or different families now live in those houses. I do not know who has survived, who is in prison or who is, as I am, an exile. I feel as if part of my past has been erased, and that I am unable to connect my present to the experiences I had before leaving my country. Nor have I been able to speak with my friends from high school because no one is permitted to attend a party at night, past curfew. They are suspicious of large gatherings, and my family fears that if we have people over to our house, they will come and interrogate me about my departure from Chile after the coup. Although my father is a supporter of Pinochet and thus, according to them, I am protected, they are still afraid, they fear everything, as do all the inhabitants of our crushed homeland.

I feel I have been destroyed by seeing this pathetic reality. This is not the Chile that I left behind in 1974. This is not the Chile where you and I, years ago, walked together along the beaches daydreaming about the visions we had of our free future. Marjorie, I want you to also realize that this is no longer our homeland about which we dream every day in our adoptive country in the North.

Yesterday I spent almost all afternoon in the General Cemetery of Santiago in front of the niche of my brother Hugo. I sat on an empty bench and, without taking my eyes off the gravestone bearing my brother's name, I spoke to him silently. I told him of my wanderings in that foreign land and I told him of his beloved Chile. I said that I still did not understand why he left us, but I knew his spirit had not died, that he was with me every day, an inseparable part of my own soul. I talked about the sorrow I felt for Chile and my people, and I asked that he, who had more power than we, from wherever he might be now, please guide us in some way and use whatever strength he had to help us make sense of this tragedy. When the sun began to set and the afternoon began to change color, I remembered his voice and I could hear him, so clearly, as I had heard him before he died. He told me so many things, and I slowly started to understand the moments of my wandering . . . and I stayed there listening to him until a police officer interrupted me and told me that they were going to close the cemetery, and that I had to leave. I got up from the bench and said good-bye to Hugo, touching the gravestone with both my hands. It was hot—but although the sun had covered it for part of the day, I am convinced that the warmth came from Hugo's spirit that had come to visit me all afternoon, to make me understand that those we loved so much never die, they are only far away.

Today I have gotten up early so I could write to you, and also to talk with my mother and tell her that I am returning to the USA. I will again attempt to make a life there, and I am beginning to think about how that country will be my new homeland, because I cannot live with rifles pointed at my back and with fear in my eyes. I am returning to the USA where I will always be an immigrant, without my own horizon, without my land, dreaming about my return to a country that exists only as a blurred memory.

Thinking of you,
Emma

✳

August 19, 1976
Reno, Nevada

Dear Marjorie,

I was happy to find out that you are writing poetry again. The story you told me of your professor—the man who said you should not write anymore and you should devote yourself to a more "feminine" activity—infuriated me! I could not believe that we still have to face those attacks. Not only must we overcome discrimination as Latinos in this country, but along with that we have to face the different way we're treated as women. Do you suppose we will overcome this double disadvantage someday?

Your story has filled me with even more desire to write. I am writing poetry about the events in 1973 in Chile, and the nostalgia of the profound space it left between my past and what is now my present. Writing helps my own wounds heal a little, and allows me to denounce the cruelties of the dictatorship to a world that is still ignorant of what our brothers endure in Chile.

I am continuing my studies of photography, and the photographic art is helping me re-create what I see during my trips and then transform it into a parallel, imagined reality. It is difficult to absorb all my experiences here in this country and not be unmoved by changes in perspective. My life still seems to be a dream, a bad dream perhaps, from which I am going to awaken someday, in some place where I will find my own space.

This is the last week I will work at the Mexican restaurant. I have a teaching assistantship at the University of Nevada in Reno, and I will teach Spanish to first-year students while I study for my master's degree. The owners of this restaurant have helped me very much, but this reality has opened my eyes to experiences so distinct from my own that I am now counting the hours left at this job. As you know, our world in Chile was protected, limited, and innocent, but I now have been witness to so many things that I am finding it difficult to understand my life from these new viewpoints.

Here in Reno I have been able to get a close look at a world I never dreamed could have existed, one that I would have imagined could only be created in the movies. This city is awake twenty-four hours a day, 365 days a year, and anything you can imagine can be found here. Each human being is a world. I met a woman, a coworker, who is from Bolivia. She came to this city with a shipment of cocaine that her own father had packed into tubes of toothpaste, creams, and all kinds of products for women. This woman passed through the airport with three sisters, smuggling an enormous amount of illegal drugs (her father not only got them visas with the help of a North American trafficker, but also had one of the girls marry the drug trafficker), and that way he earned enough money to buy property in La Paz, Bolivia. I knew nothing of her background until she invited me to eat lunch at her mobile home on a day we were both off work. When I entered her house, I realized that all around she had a certain kind of plant, like delicate ferns, and lamps that gave off a very bright light that made the plants' intense green color stand out even more. Like an idiot, I asked what kind of plant it was, and if I could have a cutting in order to grow it in my apartment. The woman stared at me, her face showing enormous surprise, and began to laugh hysterically at me. She told me that she knew I was a little naive, but she could not believe that I had never seen a marijuana plant before. When she stopped laughing, she explained that she grew marijuana and sold it to a distributor in San Francisco. That same day, she recounted her unforgettable experience of crossing into the United States with the shipment of cocaine. Marjorie, you can't imagine how afraid I was. While I listened to her talk about drug trafficking, I looked around me at all those marijuana plants and I felt they were very alive, like the carnivorous plants in the jungle. I looked at them and thought that at any moment the FBI would burst through the door, like in the movies, and they would whisk the two of us off to jail. The moment came when I could no longer tolerate the fear—I interrupted her stories and said that I was leaving and didn't want to know anything more about her or of her activities in the drug underworld. I fled her house, all the while remembering that, if this had happened in Chile, this woman would go directly to jail without a hearing and, once there, they would shoot her. I sat in my apartment wondering if I should denounce her to the authorities or if I should wait until the police found out about her by themselves without any information from me. I do not know how things are here, but according to what I have read, I nearly die from fright every time I think that the traffickers who work with her might come and take me out of my little apartment and kill me in cold blood one of these nights because of the information that I have. Now when I go to work I try to avoid the Bolivian, and I do not want to speak to anyone else about my experience either.

Among the other people I have met is a beautiful woman, twenty-four years old, with blond hair and a body that is a work of art. This woman worked sometimes as a substitute for another waitress who was in the process of getting a divorce and had to miss her shift for a few days. The girl is also a prostitute and works when they call her to "entertain" some tourist. Although you might find this strange, prostitution is legal outside the city limits, but it seems nobody respects that law. I had never met anyone who did that kind of work, so when I spent some time chatting with her and she mentioned her "little extra work on the side," I was totally surprised. She talked quite naturally about the things that her clients asked her to do, and the prices for the services that she offered. She has special rates for young men, for old men, for oral sex, and for "special orders," as she called them. Marjorie, you would have had to have been there to picture my face as she spoke to me. In our culture everything about sex is secretive and forbidden, and nobody talks about *that*, so I gawked at this woman without being able to even imagine what it was like when she talked about faking orgasms or screaming like crazy, or about the men that tied her to the bed, and of the shapes and sizes of genitals that she has had in every opening on her body. When she finished describing the details of her work and telling me how much money she earned, she looked at me with an inquisitive look on her face (surely, I thought, because I had an idiotic look on my face: I was wide-eyed, incredulous, and my mouth hung open from surprise!!), and after a pause, she asked me if I wanted to work with her on the weekends. Can you even begin to envision my face when she asked me that question? I didn't know how to answer her because I did not want to belittle her work, especially after she had given detailed descriptions of her great skill and the enormous pride she felt when she "left her clients extremely satisfied." I hesitated a little and the first thing that occurred to me to say was that I couldn't because I was studying at the university. It was a mistake to respond that way because she immediately answered back with something that I would have never imagined: she said many students in the sororities supplemented their incomes with this "extra work" on the weekends. That made me even more embarrassed and, again, trying not to offend her, the most ridiculous words I've ever uttered in my life came out of my mouth: I said that I was Catholic and I could not fornicate outside of marriage. I believe she finally realized how strange the whole topic was for me, and she told me to forget what she had said, and that another day we would finish our conversation. She never spoke to me again when she would come visit her friend in the restaurant.

I have learned many things here in this place, much more than about tacos, burritos, and enchiladas; I have learned things that I would have never seen up close in another setting. I have met marvelous people that work like animals and dream about returning to their country, educating their children, and buying a piece of land to the south of the Rio Grande. Those are people I will never forget.

Write me soon.

All the best,
Emma

✳

Dear Emma,

I am writing to you during a rainy afternoon in Viña del Mar. I have always loved this city. When the people of Santiago invade it, they sometimes mistreat it, then they abandon it, alone and silenced, as if it wished to withdraw and be renamed. The rain here on the coast is sweet and velvety. It still astonishes me to see the rain over the sea, and I have always marveled at the legends about cities of the sea and the rain. Legends that I no longer know if I invented myself or if, when I heard them, I then learned how to invent them.

As I wrote before, I received a scholarship from Indiana University to travel to Chile and interview María Luisa Bombal. Those in the Chilean literary circle have created a setting that I fear because of the danger of their tongues and the mediocrity of their being. They told me that she did not grant interviews and lived in seclusion, spent her days drinking in a house that is next door to that of her deranged cousins and a young man whom she called her secretary, an odd boy of fifteen or sixteen years of age with the face of an errant bird. However, family ties brought me to her — ties that had nothing to do with literature. They had to do with my uncle Gregorio Agosín, the dentist. María Luisa Bombal was his patient and he never charged her. She, being a very kind lady, was devoted to giving away beautiful books of her own prose or that of her friends but, clearly, always autographed by her. The truth is that she did not have the money with which to pay my uncle for the consultation. My uncle asked her and, after extraordinary efforts, she granted me an interview. So it was that on a night filled with storms and multicolored lightning, I went to the home of María Luisa Bombal. I am customarily quite disoriented, but I sensed that I was near her house because there was only one that had a streetlight, twinkling delicately, very languid and melancholic. It was something out of a Bergman movie in the middle of the Southern Hemisphere.

María Luisa Bombal received me, dressed completely in black and wearing a silver medallion in the shape of an immense cross. I saw her and heard her slow, rhythmic voice, a powerful, soft voice that caressed me and made me smile. From that moment on, I knew I had penetrated the privileged realms of magic and dreams. I felt she was a friend because her speech was that of poetry and had nothing to do with the fatuous things of the world. Her voice was something like the firefly that played with the heroines who dwelled in southern Chile along the Malloco River; you might remember that it appears in many of her tales, for example that of María Griselda. Do you remember her? She was the heroine captivated by her own beauty; the one who talked with the toads that fell in love with her. I remember that you preferred to read the works of Marta Brunet.

I spent several hours at that first encounter, and it seems as if it took place yesterday. We walked up a perpendicular, labyrinthian stairway and there she was, like one of the legends I heard told during rainy days. She told me that even blindfolded she could find her way through her city of Viña del Mar. So, with her tone that is between poetry and myth, we two were able to arrive at an understanding, to feel that our voices were like the pulsing of the wind, or of time.

That is how that afternoon transpired. It was repeated each afternoon during the winter in Viña del Mar. I interned myself in that space of women who are translucent inhabitants of forests and the back of beyond, and I allowed myself to be carried by her gestures and her rituals, like that of closing all the blinds in the house as night was falling so as to prevent the spirits of María Griselda or La Amortajada from overhearing all that she was writing. Everything she imagined existed outside the sphere of reality. With her, Emma, I had my first lessons as a writer and I came to feel immensely happy. I surrendered myself to that faith that permits the entrance to the adverse and to the surreal, to the gift of the imagination.

I am happy, Emma, that she is our María Luisa Bombal, my

first entrance to the written word. It makes me proud that she is from Chile and that soon, far away, in the middle of the United States, my voice and my words will restore her. I admit that her sadness worries me, as well as her absence due to what the critics call her scanty presence in our national culture. I am concerned because she can barely survive, she is in poor health and can barely make ends meet, and I know that the same as La Amortajada, she will not be tempted by the desire to live again. She will be like Gabriela, honored in the land of the bulls, but not in that of the pious. Will that also be our future?

Magi

❋

July 1977

My dear Emma:

I never thought I would be writing you again so soon. I wanted to tell you that a few hours ago the telephone rang here in our apartment in Bloomington, and my papá informed me that my grandfather had died. As always, dearest Emma, death is inopportune and unforeseen. When all is said and done, death is always present in our lives. The passing of my Opapá represents the loss of my companion of dreams and journeys, of my own historian, but more than anything, a dearly beloved friend.

For a long time, my grandfather occupied a central part of my life. I was not only his granddaughter, I accompanied him on his inner journeys. Through him, I learned how to love life, the unexpected, and the uncertain. As I've told you, my grandfather was a true Viennese gentleman. He treated the women in his house courteously and with great deference. My grandmother Chepita, whom you love and know so well, never managed to understand the quixotisms of her José. She was obsessed with bills, the precision of mathematics, and she had a green notebook in which she recorded not his life but instead how much my grandfather owed.

José would laugh and continued donating money to the Hebrew school, to the nuns, and above all, to the funeral association that he himself helped to establish. You might say that José Halpern was devotedly concerned about the destination of the dead, and thus in life he donated a lot of money to the association.

I have told you many things about José. He was already a hippie at the beginning of the century. He was a marvelous visionary, a spectacular being. Together we used to stroll on Sundays. We always walked arm-in-arm and would imagine what was not and what could not be, as if we were two children looking at the world upside down. Once he told me that the Andes mountains were a beautiful cake, and in the same instant he said that people believed in me and that I should be responsible for my promises and my achievements.

My thoughts are spinning. John is at my side; he is with me because he also loved and continues loving him. He used to tell me that my grandfather looked like Albert Einstein with his beautiful translucent hair, as if the moon were descending very softly onto his skin.

It will be difficult living without the hope of having him by my side. You know, Emma, my grandparents lived across the street from our house, and I would leave our house with a small blue suitcase and tell my sister, "I'm leaving home." Then I would go stay with Grandmother Chepi and Grandfather José. After a while I would become bored and would return home, loudly announcing upon my arrival: "I'm home. Here I am!"

My grandfather never talked about his marvelous achievements nor, following the instructions of the Talmud, did he ever tell others about his charitable works. He aided many people during the disastrous years of the war. Many of the refugees did not know what to do, where to live, or how to protect themselves from the bleakness and pain. José Halpern offered them help. He gave them his hand, a kiss on the cheek, and some flowers—but moreover he offered them the possibility of a life still worthy of respect and full of wonder.

Today while I am writing you, it gives me pleasure to invoke him and tell you so many things about him during these long, sad hours when my memories are my only solace.

Magi

✳

Dear Emma,

I was married a week ago. Are you surprised? Are you angry because I didn't let you know about it? Are you shocked or are you laughing? The truth is that I didn't have a very clear idea about marriage. Honestly, I preferred to spend entire nights gazing at the stars with an imaginary telescope or writing poems by candle-light and the scent of lavender. But suddenly I saw a flash of light and I told myself, "You should marry John Wiggins." Now I can say I am English. The simple truth is, Emma, that I am in love with this gorgeous man that, in spite of being named John, has the face of an Arab. He is a wonderful guy, a true self-made man. He was the first in his family to attend college and is very different from the other men I have had the opportunity to know, men for whom I only existed in order to be with them and feed their egos. I love John madly and don't ask me why because that is the way love is.

My parents have known him for two years, but they were also surprised when I told them that I was getting married so soon be-cause I wanted a small wedding. So it was, in a few seconds we began to organize the wedding, to think about what to do and not do, whom to invite and whom to exclude . . .

My mother, who is a true empresario (remember she organized the first garage sale in Chile), began to call her Hispanic friends, and in less than two days they began preparing the food: beans, tortillas, salsas, shellfish, pork, kosher chicken, and much more. A very eclectic and very esoteric wedding, and it filled me with a greatly sublime happiness. Then, Emma, the most beautiful thing was that we were wed according to our faith (I don't like to say Jewish religion) under a *chuppah,* which is like an awning that was used in ancient times—it symbolizes the desert and the endless travels through the sands—and John and I heard the breeze of God under this blue awning.

Some dear friends supported it as I walked joyfully underneath. A gentleman played music of Segovia underneath our tree . . . the tree by which John and I kissed for the first time. And there was John, my gringo Omar Sharif, awaiting me. He nearly fainted due to the tremendous danger he faced—that is, marrying me!

The party was very cheerful, and we played Latin, Hebrew, and gringo music. I experienced a great sadness as my father said farewell to me. We both sensed that I would never return home.

That's all, Emma. Perhaps I'll send the secret details of our honeymoon . . . in a shorter, juicier letter. We will drive to Bloomington, Indiana, where John will continue with his physics courses, and I with my beloved poetry and literature.

Your dear friend, now your dear married friend,
Magi

✳

February 1978

Dear Emma,

I am writing you from Bloomington, Indiana, at the beginning of a ferocious winter. It is my first year in graduate school, and I have so much to tell you. Bloomington is a town of gently rolling, golden hills—not as majestic as our mountain range, but our gaze becomes accustomed to this landscape. There were many times in Chile when I felt insignificant as I beheld the majesty of those irreverent and insolent peaks. My body has become comfortable in the Midwest of the United States, but I believe what has most soothed my existence is I have confronted this perennial situation of feeling myself apart, a foreigner marked by her accent and by memories radically different from those of the others.

I have found companionship in some professors who lived in Chile in the seventies, an epoch that is glorified here and during which we were young girls. But anyway, we managed to have a happy childhood. I have a teacher who wrote the first book about

AMIGAS

Chilean literary criticism. I admire him very much because he does not have an imperialist outlook about the world around us. There is another professor that studied in the Institute of Chilean Literature. He loves Neruda, Pedro Lastra, and María Luisa Bombal.

I am fearful, Emma, because it seems I am living the history of our Chile through others — I will never be able to go to the cafes of Santiago and experience the nocturnal life, the little Bohemia, of our so-called intellectuals. I sense that my past remains suspended in a memory that is constantly becoming more transparent, more tenuous, almost ineffable. But being with these teachers gladdens me. It makes me feel more important, perhaps because they transform me into an exotic character, and better loved.

There are very few Chileans in Indiana. Those that are here already consider me a foreigner. That is to say, even among them I feel that difference about which I told you. I am Jewish, I went to Jewish schools. I did not attend a Chilean university and that, in a way, gives us a point of commonality. As you might see, I am trying to understand myself here, bobbing on a seesaw as I try to comprehend what I left behind and what I am creating.

I have a Peruvian professor. He always talks about the wars between Peru and Chile. He tells me that Chilean women are renowned as prostitutes and that my poetry leaves much to be desired. I listen respectfully, accustomed to demonstrating the calm and deferential obedience that I was taught in school by the nuns, as well as by my mother and grandmothers. It hurts when I remember what he said about the [wars between our countries] and the Chilean prostitutes. I smile and always blush.

The positive aspect is the marvelous library and the music, the sounds emitted from every pore of this city, and the fact that I married a foreigner who reminded me, from the first time that I saw him, of Omar Sharif, with his marvelous Arab face . . . which are forbidden faces, don't you think?

This experience of books, studies, and research I imagine is new for you also. We are lacking in materials and in our studies, but that does not prevent my astonishment at the [seemingly limitless] possibilities that this country offers, especially an unequaled access to information. However, behind all this one sees the out-line of an immense solitude, a lack of words and speech.

When do you think we will see each other? You are so far away and I am here in the middle of the country with very little money. These letters will have to be our only support—at least they are for me.

I love you awfully,

Marjorie

✳

July 20, 1979
Santiago, Chile

Dear Marjorie:

I am sorry you had to return to the USA so soon, I would have liked to spend more time with you on this project.

Very early in the morning I left my mother's house and re-turned to the National Vicariate to meet with those amazing women who have discovered a way to denounce this cruel dicta-torship. I looked forward to meeting with the *arpilleristas* so I could take more photos and continue listening to their stories. I do not know at times which is better: to photograph the images, or allow their stories to be the testimony of what is happening in Chile and write the oral histories. For days I have been taking photos, mostly of their hands and parts of their bodies—they don't want their faces photographed because they are afraid that some-body might recognize them, and then they might be detained for their subversive activity—sewing scraps of fabric into scenes that all Chileans have witnessed but cannot depict or discuss openly because of the relentless censorship and fear. They use their hand-sewn *arpilleras* as protest against the dictatorship and as a de-nouncement of the violation of human rights.

I spend hours thinking of the stories that the women have told me, and I experience a combination of feelings. I feel enormous sorrow for the tragedy that they live, and there are moments in which I experience a profound sense of guilt because you and I managed to escape alive, and we are yet leading privileged lives because our situation in the United States is better than what they could ever hope to have here.

I do not have any children, but I can understand the tremendous grief that these women feel because they have lost their sons and daughters. But worse yet is that they did not see their children die, but rather they only know that they have disappeared and nobody knows how, when, or where they might have died. It is the same sorrow felt by the women who have lost their husbands or brothers or sisters who have disappeared under this horrible dictatorship. I have spent a lot of time speaking with all of them, and although they did not want to trust me at first—because they did not understand why we would want to know their stories—we now share our experiences as if we had known each other all our lives. One of the stories I heard today became forever engraved upon my memory: Violeta's story. She is the only single woman in the group because she lived with her partner without getting married, and that left her a branded woman. The other women find it difficult to understand why she never married and "lived in sin" with a man, defying the laws of God and society. Moreover, Violeta was a member of the Chilean Socialist Party, and her family disowned her for being a rebel with regard to politics and customs. I have spent hours with Violeta and already know her life so well that I almost have it memorized. One day I want to write down all of this, but for the moment I do not want to bring a tape recorder to our meetings because if they detain me in the street and arrest me, the less evidence I have of our "subversive" activity the safer our future. At night when I return to the house, I write a few pages and fall asleep thinking of their stories, and how we will tell these stories to the world. Violeta is an invincible woman and has survived the impossible. Since she was in high school she has been an activist. She marched in the teachers' strikes and participated in the Worker's Union every chance she could. When she met her partner, she began to work in the Socialist Party, and she dedicated every waking hour to organizing groups of women workers, registering them to vote, and taking them to the polling places on election days. With great pride, she tells me of how those women elected Salvador Allende and fought to defend their government against the attacks from the right. But she also describes the tremendous horror that she has experienced after the military coup. She and her partner hid when soldiers came to their house in the middle of the night. As soon as they heard the bangs on the door, they ran through their patio to their neighbors' house, and when the soldiers left they escaped in a taxi. They went into hiding in the house of some friends until the soldiers leveled that house and carried off the men—they left [Violeta and another woman by themselves] after brutally beating them. But the following night the soldiers returned and, on the pretext of looking for secret documents in the house, they raped the two women. Violeta was so badly beaten that when she regained consciousness her friend called the emergency medical service and they took her to the hospital. At the hospital, nobody wanted to believe their story because nobody, nobody, would dare accuse soldiers of any sort of crime, because those men "defend our country from the leftist threat," and they don't attack our people, they defend the homeland and the citizens: and that is the official history of Chile. Since that time, Violeta has been living in one house and then another, with the immense fear that someday, in some secret place, they will find her again and this time they will not rape her but she will disappear like her boyfriend, and like the other woman, her *compañera* who was the only witness there that night and the person who called the ambulance to denounce the crime. Violeta survived that night, wounded in body and soul. Her friend disappeared.

Marjorie, these are the other histories, the extensions of the stories that you and I listened to in the Vicariate, and that I continue hearing in the poor barrios. I wish you could have been here and we could have visited these places together. Yesterday while I met with a group of *arpilleristas* in a humble church in the La Pincoya barrio, one of the volunteer women of the church ran to warn us that two military vans were coming slowly down the main street of the barrio. In a matter of seconds, they grabbed me by my arm and pushed me out to the patio, and from there to the railing below and, running with me, they guided me through several patios of the houses, between hens, dogs, and cats, onto a side street, where they put me in an old taxi that was parked in front of one of the homes. After a few minutes the driver arrived and he asked the address where I wanted to be taken, and without saying a word about the matter he took me to my mother's house. These women are so very organized, and it is in this way that they protect those who come to aid them in their search for their missing relatives. I have learned very much from all this, Marjorie. As yet, I cannot understand how this country has [enraged] our women and why it continues to attack them so brutally. They have taken their children, their husbands, their brothers and sisters, and everything that comprised an integral part of their lives, and now that [this regime has] forced the women to go out into the street to protest, they are branded with the names of "rebels," "subversives," "communists," and other things.

I would like to remain here in Chile so I could work with women who belong to a group of relatives of the detained and disappeared, but I know how difficult it would be with the resistance inside of Chile, and I could end up detained like the others who are already suffering the consequences of their activities. I believe we could do more from the outside for these women and for Chile, and perhaps we will return someday when one is not in danger for following a different political ideology. Meanwhile, let's try to help them with their work of embroidering and making tapestries so that they can denounce to the world the injustices that exist in Chile. Let's continue this fight, albeit from a distance, and we will smuggle all the *arpilleras* we can out of the country. We will write these histories, we will give talks about their lives, and we will do everything possible so that the struggle of these women is not in vain. I will telephone you as soon as I arrive in the USA. In the meantime, send me positive vibrations so that [I] don't [also disappear] amidst this terror.

All my best,
Emma

※

Dear Emma,

I have returned this winter to Isla Negra. I do not know the reason for this habit of mine of choosing certain sites to commemorate moments in the uncertain passage of time. But I needed to return, like someone who returns to past loves that are as yet unresolved and longs to recognize the texture of the flames, the pleasure of what was beautiful.

Many times I have told you that my mother and I would take long walks from our modest house in Quisco to Isla Negra in the afternoon, where the coast extended before us with its most generous magnitude. The sky, like the sun, created alliances of colors, violet and crimson. Nowhere else have I seen sunsets like those in Quisco and Isla Negra, or perhaps they are the memories of happier years and thus I long for repetitions of a lost time.

I travel along the path of memory like a Penelope who wishes to return to the Ithaca of her childhood. I recognize certain stones, small and large, certain winding roads that murmur the sounds of their dread in the night. I also remember an unworried stroll, balancing myself on my mother's arm, confusing our coppery hair. We would walk without saying anything or simply singing.

It is only now that I understand that this was happiness: an unhurried walk, a breeze on sunny days, a forest that spoke and forever bordered the sea. In moments of intense desperation I return to the coast, to those walks, and I breathe deeply. I assure myself that no matter the phase of my life, happiness is close at hand.

Now I walk alone to the island. My hair is confused like that of Medusa. My mother no longer returns to Chile with the same frequency. We have become an American family. We have acquired all their defects and their few virtues. My sister and I do not even visit one another. My nephews are unknown to me. I wonder if everything would have been different if we had remained in Chile . . . or perhaps not.

During the winter on the island, as Neruda described in his autobiography, everything flourishes and it is filled with yellow flowers. The tourists have disappeared and I hear a profound silence, a silence that contains a history. Here lived Don Pablo. He wrote his poems in large notebooks with green ink. Here lived Violeta Parra in the thirties, in a little fisherman's cabin. A great part of the cultural history of Chile occurred here, very near to that which our eyes behold. But how little we know about our history, about the elaborations of our town.

I approach the stone path that leads to the house of Neruda. I have passed near it often. I have seen it from afar. Once he wrote me a poem that I still have, and he told me that I had the voice of a bell. There is no one in the house of the poet. All stands still and dark, as if a great mourning possesses every corner. My body is then rainfall, lamentation, flood.

The house of Neruda is surrounded by immense doors with signs that say "No sightseeing. Entry is prohibited." The red doorbell does not ring, gone are the [artists and writers] that I visited before, when the house was illuminated. They probably also weep in silence.

I am filled with the desire to telephone you, to write to you, and if only I could embrace you, to be close to you like we used to be on Sundays. You, after your long visit to church, and I after being so alone. On Sundays I would wait for my friends in the neighborhood to return from church and I'd hope that one of them would dare, although it might be only for a few minutes, to play with the Jewish witch.

Emma, our country is a long, fragile, interrupted silence, a cemetery of large and small deaths. I return to the main road, now destroyed. I will take the bus that will carry me to the home of my grandmother in Valparaiso, where my family, the great majority of it, believes that thus it should be, that it is necessary to murder to maintain order in the families and peace in the nation. I will not be able to speak with any of them, and so I will end this dark day, [hoping that soon all our dark days will cease.]

I love you,
Marjorie

✳

August 20, 1980
Reno, Nevada

Dear Marjorie,

I received your letter from Argentina in which you tell me that you are working with the women of La Plaza de Mayo in a project similar to ours in Chile. You have no idea how glad I am to know that you continue to be so committed to the human rights cause. We cannot remain silent in the face of the atrocities that are being committed in Latin America—above all, those committed against women. The militarist culture that has been instituted in our countries has violated the precarious rights that women have achieved through tremendous effort. The dictatorships have erased the inroads that women had gained through their struggle. [The regimes are] not making changes through the political process by means of the vote, but by absolutely prohibiting that women participate in the political organizations of our countries. I personally feel that one of the many ways that a woman's destiny is being controlled is this return to the archaic patterns of years past, in which the place of women in society means to be a mother, wife, and housekeeper, and nothing more. The dictatorships want to establish a regime in which women are denied participation in any political, social, and economic change. Keep the women at home and tied to the foot of the bed!! Nobody wants to talk about legislation for abortion or divorce. Nobody wants women to receive the same salary as men for doing the same work. But the most tragic thing is that they mutilate women's lives when they take their children and kill them. The dictatorship wants mothers, but it seems only silent mothers after they have stolen their children and made them disappear. [This, by itself, is reason enough] to continue this struggle so that they don't take away what we have achieved up to now. Women must continue organizing themselves to defeat the power of the dictatorships and not lose their power in the elections, in the courts, and most importantly in the legislation that affects our lives. But we must also continue supporting a woman's right to a better education, better working conditions, and a comparable salary.

It infuriates me to read what the conservative press says about the mothers of La Plaza de Mayo. They call them "the crazy women of La Plaza de Mayo," and they don't respect them as human beings who are protesting injustices and abuses. They consider them "politicized women" and "revolutionaries." The irony is that the soldiers who say this are the ones who made them that way. They killed their children!! And so they go out into the street to demand answers about the disappearance of their [sons and daughters]. But beyond this justification for their acts, I wonder, Marjorie: is it so terrible that women are political or rebellious??

While you are in Argentina working on that [remarkable] project, I am packing up my bags and leaving Reno. As you surely expected from our telephone conversation, I left Michael and I have asked for a divorce. I also received an acceptance letter from the doctoral program at the University of California in Davis, and I have indeed decided to continue the doctorate there. A month passed before I had the courage to call Chile and give the news to my family. My father accepted it and offered me his help, but my mother was horror-struck at the thought that I would be the first person in the history of our family to get divorced. After our telephone conversation, she wrote me and reminded me that according to the teachings of the Catholic Church, with which we had been inculcated from childhood, the vow of marriage was for the rest of our lives . . . "what God has joined together let no man put apart." Also, she told me to write to the pope and request a special annulment so that in case I marry again, I won't commit adultery. At the end of her letter she told me that only the immediate family must know about this and the others, including our friends, should not know for the time being. I do not understand the importance of this secrecy and why they are humiliated by my actions. I think they would have been happier if I had told them that my marriage was a disaster but because of the Church and what people would say, I would remain married forever. It was difficult to come to this decision and to go forward, because I am very afraid to live alone in this country or to return to Chile as a "divorced woman." The stigma that exists in our countries is difficult to overcome. According to the conventions of our society, men always get divorced for a good reason: their wives got fat, their wives don't like to have sex, they found a younger and more understanding woman, personal incompatibility, or simply that they are suffering a midlife crisis. But all those reasons identify and depict the men as VICTIMS. However, the woman that requests a divorce is harshly criticized in other ways. She is attacked because she has not considered the children, they suspect that she is an adultress, they say she wants a divorce so she can sleep around, etc., etc. All these accusations transform her into a BAD WOMAN. It is always the same, one set of rules for the men and a completely different set for the women. Since I was married in Chile and there is no divorce in that country, I will forever carry the brand of being a single but married woman. Another irony!! All this makes me bitter but will not alter my decision to get divorced and go live alone in California. I hope to spend more time writing and studying, but I will also participate somehow in politics and in community organizations, as I have done here in Nevada.

Good luck during the final weeks of your project. Write me and call me if you are able before you leave.

Best wishes,
Emma

August 1981
Venecia, Italy

Dear Marjorie,

I am still enjoying Italy. This country has not only unearthed memories of Grandfather Silvestre, but also has awakened in me dormant feelings and has made me think again about the love of a man. The man is John, the one I mentioned to you before. He graduated from our university and came to study in Europe for the summer before going on to graduate school in Riverside, California. Through the help of my assistant, who is also my traveling companion, he found out about our itinerary in Europe and decided to wait for me somewhere and surprise me with a reunion. After weeks of backpacking, little sleep, trains, few baths, and a total negligence of my physical appearance, when I got off the train that arrived from Florence to Venice I saw, standing up at a little table in an outdoor cafe, John. The first thought that occurred to me was to run in the opposite direction and hide so that he wouldn't see me, but when I finally reacted, I decided to continue walking toward him. My steps seemed to last forever and the distance did not shorten, while my legs trembled uncontrollably and my pulse galloped like a frightened horse. When we were finally face-to-face, I tried to control my happiness and, with an almost natural indifference, I extended my hand and greeted him as if we were only distant friends. We sat down in the cafe and he told me that the previous week he had traveled from Austria to Venice in order to await every train coming from Florence so that he might find me. I was deeply moved by his story, but I tried not to [reveal] the slightest emotion, [I didn't want him to know how] his words were touching my heart. We spent the rest of the day walking through the streets filled with tourists and, at dusk, after having dinner, we rode in a gondola through the channels of the city in the twilight. We conversed about thousands of things, and I was surprised by the limitless capacity he had to listen and enjoy each comment, each sentence, each word that left another person's mouth. When he spoke, it was impossible for me to concentrate on his words because I constantly lost myself in his blue eyes and he transported me in silence to a world of uncontrollable passions. In one moment of the trip, between those dark waters and the limpid night, he took me in his arms and pressed me to him, and both of us fell silent. A part of me wanted to escape those strong, sure arms, but another part of me, more powerful than the first, wanted to stay there forever. I wanted to leave his arms so he wouldn't realize that my whole body was trembling and my hands were wet with perspiration. But I wanted to remain so that at last he might kiss me, kiss me as I had imagined he would kiss me, surely as no one had ever kissed me before. Toward the end of our tour, he took my face in his hands and tried to give me the kiss I had longed for. We looked at each other for a few seconds, and then I turned my face because I had an awful fear of surrendering myself to that kiss. He did not insist, and during the rest of our gondola ride he did not put his arm around my shoulders again. Afterward, we walked through those small lanes that seem imagined streets, until we arrived at the hotel. The hotel is small and the rooms seem to rotate around the old, twisted, wooden stairway. We reached the second floor where my room is located, and when we were in front of my door he asked me if he could come in for a few minutes. I had the same internal struggle that I had in the gondola, and the part of me filled with questions without answers triumphed again, and I told him no, I preferred to be alone that night. I said good-bye, closed the door, and waited with my back pressed to the door listening to his steps. Each stair that he descended gave me a terrible feeling of despair, of wanting to leave my room [and go after] him and ask him to stay with me that night. But as you can already guess, I didn't do it.

The following day I arose as early as possible, and when I went downstairs to eat breakfast the receptionist told me that somebody had left a letter for me. The letter was from John. He told me that he was returning to Austria to finish his German course and if I wished I could visit him before finishing my trip. Can you imagine my surprise? We spent only a day together in this city filled with romantic places and then he leaves without even saying good-bye. I do not know what I am going to do. Now I am more confused than ever. I feel an enormous attraction for this man, but I have a terrible fear of falling in love and becoming one of those women who cannot live without the constant presence of her spouse. I want to travel, write, study, and continue following my free spirit, without tying it to anything or anyone.

The experience with this man has prompted me to write a ton of poems, some good and others full of an absurd romanticism, adolescent and stupid, that surely will never, ever be published. Four days have passed since he left, and I am still dreaming about this city and am consumed by doubt.

I will spend a few days writing and taking photos in Venice, and from here I go to France. I believe that I will return to California at the end of September in order to finish writing a work for a conference in Kentucky. Take care and don't work too much.

Love,
Emma

✳

October 15, 1982
California

Dear Marjorie,

Living in California has been marvelous but being a graduate student in this university has been quite a different experience than I had expected. I have to teach two classes of Spanish, and in the afternoon I attend courses. I love teaching, but what I have learned about the academic world is extremely alarming. There exists little respect for women, and this has created a subworld so that instead of an academic institution, it seems more like a soap opera done in poor taste. Almost all the students studying for a master's or Ph.D. are women, and the professors are all men. The way they treat the students is incredible. There is a literature professor from Latin America who makes comments about the "good-looking legs" of the women who wear short skirts and the bust size of the others. All his comments are sexual. There are other professors who make fun of two homosexuals who are members of their faculty. Their jokes always refer to other men being careful—not to turn your back on them in the elevator because they'll go for your ass, or not going to urinate when they are in the bathroom because they might grab your penis. This creates an atmosphere of paranoia that forces the students who are homosexuals to hide their sexuality, fearing the jeers or reprisals of the professors. All these joking attacks against the homosexuals I find repugnant. These intellectuals hide themselves in their supposed castles of wisdom, and they believe themselves superior to [everyone else], but they are the most backward and insensitive beings I have met in this country.

In this atmosphere where, apparently, the concept of "sexual harassment" is unknown, the abuses of power are difficult to accept and impossible to stop. There are several professors who have taken graduate students as lovers. The professors are married, as are some of the female students. These professors are the chairs of the exam committee or the thesis directors for the women. All the other students know what is happening but we participate through our collective, obligatory silence, fearing the reprisals.

A couple of months ago a visiting professor, who had the key to [a colleague's] office, after knocking on the door without any response, used the key and opened the door. What a tremendous surprise he got when he saw that sprawled on the desk of his colleague he didn't find dissertation chapters or books or exams, but rather the brown buttocks of a female student with her legs wide open, making love with her devoted thesis director. Both teacher and pupil were as they had entered this world, without a stitch of clothing to cover the parts that had carried them to that erotic conference. The professor kept his body on top of his student to prevent exposing her intimate parts to the visitor. The professor who had indiscreetly interrupted their "meeting" quickly turned out the light and exited the office without saying a single word. That night he called my apartment and told me in detail what he had seen and asked if I knew of their sinful romance. I listened to him without offering him my opinion and I refused to give him any information I had about the situation. I had learned, and continue learning, that silence is your best friend in graduate school. But I had learned little about how to protect myself from the advances of those "in charge."

Marjorie, you aren't going to believe this, but my turn came.

As I've told you, my area of specialization was Latin American poetry, but since the [scandal] began about my committee chair and his student-lover, the plans of many of the women who were working with that professor drastically changed. The group divided itself into those who had helped him with his love affairs and those he believed (according to his own paranoia) had not supported him. I fell into the group that he began to hate, and since the department had already been transformed into a nest of vipers, I opted to change my specialization. It was terrible to alter my dreams because of the lack of professionalism that exists between these "academics." I thought that the only way to finish my blasted thesis and leave here soon would be to search out one of the older—and thus less "amorous"—professors with whom to work in my new specialization and receive the degree I expected.

I proposed a new project, and my new chair accepted it from me with a few minor changes. The number of changes increased and the days became weeks, until one day he called me and asked me to bring my project to his office after classes that night. I went to his office, and he told me that he would not approve the project and I had to begin writing on another topic, and he would help me with the research after classes ended and spring vacation began. I was indignant at having wasted all that time, but I was cheered when I heard his generous offer of help. His "offer" began with an invitation to have dinner with him in a restaurant and then became daily calls to my apartment. After going out with him once, just to be courteous, I explained to him that his invitations made me feel uncomfortable and I would not go out to dinner with him again. He very cordially accepted my explanations and, as the vacation ended, he approved my project and told me that I could begin writing the first chapter. When I finished it, he asked me to bring it to his house because he did not plan to be in his office for several days. I went to his house and the drama began. He had me wait in the living room, and after a few minutes he took out a bottle of whiskey and offered me a drink. Very amiably, so as not to anger him, I said I did not want to drink anything because I had to study later. Without saying anything more, he sat down beside me and tried to touch my breasts with both his hands and, at the same time, he began to say that he wanted to make love to me and he knew that was what I wanted also. I jumped up from the chair and he grabbed my arms and tried to kiss me. His mouth reeked of a horrible smell of alcohol and onions that nauseated me. I leapt from behind the chair and ran toward the dining room, and there began the most comical of his entreaties, because he insisted that we had to make love right there on the floor of that room because he had drunk so much he could not maintain his balance or continue chasing me. It was a horrible situation because he would not permit me to get to the door and did not listen to my explanations—until I started to scream so loudly from sheer fright that he stopped pursuing me and sat down in the dining room to tell me the details of what he planned to do with me sexually. I interrupted him and I explained to him that I was not attracted to him in the least and that, furthermore, I was deeply in love with John. He listened attentively and afterward told me that to make love we didn't need to be in love or even feel attracted to each other, and moreover if I became his lover not only would I finish my thesis sooner but also he would help me find a good position after I received my degree. He told me that I did not need to answer him at that moment, I should think about it and give him my answer when I brought him the next chapter.

I left the next chapter of my thesis in his message box with a note explaining that I would not return to his house and asked him to please not continue embarrassing me. Now I receive notes in my message box every week in which he says he is in love with me, and that I only have myself to blame because I was too provocative in his classes. I do not want to tell this to anyone because I am frightened that he will become angry and won't allow me to finish the doctorate. It is difficult to understand the abuses we must suffer when these creeps have our futures in their hands and receiving our degrees depends on them. This system must change someday—how is it possible that, after taking the classes and passing the exam, everything else is in the hands of one person? Now I understand the meaning of sexual harassment because the power that these individuals have over us allows them to do whatever they want with our bodies and our fates.

Marjorie, I have no idea how I am going to finish my thesis with this man making my life impossible. What can I do? With whom should I speak? Should I transfer to another university? And waste all these years? I know that you have had similar experiences and you are one of the few people who can give me advice about this problem.

Write me soon.

Love,
Emma

June 1983

Dear Emma,

A couple of days ago I arrived in Buenos Aires, and I cannot explain to you the intense feelings I experience in the presence of this city. I carry with me all the letters that we have exchanged over the years, especially those that you wrote me from Mendoza. I feel accompanied by those words, as if by the presence of benevolent fairies while here in this city that crackles with the boots of police and the sounds of death.

This is not the first time I have visited this city that longs to be another Paris and truly could be so. I returned with my grandmother many years ago, when I was one of those young people impassioned by literature and writers, and I dedicated all my time to looking for them so I could talk with them, to caress their books and their words. Now I myself have become one of them, and I prefer the company of others, nobler and simpler, whose occupations are not those of letters. In that year of 1972, I met Elvira Or-phée, Jorge Luis Borges, and Marta Lynch. This was a very [spe-cial time] for me, above all because in the United States I was constantly isolated by my language and my culture.

I believe that those meetings with men and women committed to the task of the words had an impact on me; even today I feel and understand it. However, my journey to Buenos Aires this time has taken on another dimension. As you are aware, Emma, the tragic history of our countries has obliged us to do other things, and we two have embraced political activism as the most profound of all vocations. I have come to write about the Mothers of La Plaza de Mayo. It sounds very presumptuous to say it in that manner: *I* came to write about *them*, extraordinary women whose voices are so powerful that they have no need of writing. Nonetheless, I have been wanting to come here, as if an irresistible force drew me to Buenos Aires. I am not quite certain what I will do. Like many of my writings or poems, I need an idea that gestates very deeply within me and then I embark upon it with a passion that will per-mit nothing less than to see it through to the end. I feel that it is the way my obsession manifests itself. It is a passion that invades me. Such are the realms of words and obsessions that besiege us but do not watch over us.

I am very interested in writing about one of the women whose life has touched me very deeply. The first time I saw her was on Dan Rather's *60 Minutes*, and I simply decided to do it, to throw myself into writing about her. I sent her a letter and passionately expressed this desire. I believe that [the letter] managed to con-vince her of all that she meant to me, of what I felt when I saw her and listened to her. Thus I came to know René.

She was waiting for me at the airport, and I felt that she was like a beloved aunt who had always known me. I realized very clearly then the [emptiness] I had felt in the zones of affection, the lack of intimacy I suffered in the United States. I felt so alone in that America in the North and yet here, with a stranger, it was as if I had returned home.

René Eppelbaum is one of the founders of the Mothers of La Plaza de Mayo. The fourteen women who met in the plaza decided to create this women's movement whose quest would be for not only their own children, but also all those children that had disappeared in Argentina—something, you know, that has had repercussions in the [entire] Southern Cone. I cannot describe to you nor explain the sensation I had upon entering her house. It was as if the presence of all of them, of the phantasmic innocent children, appeared in each corner of the house. I was very moved when I sat in the living room and saw, on the placards, the photographs of her children, showing them from their childhood until their adolescence, when they were kidnapped from the patio of their summer house in Punta del Este. Her youngest daughter is named Lila and she resembled you, Emma, with eyes like dark velvet. In fact, Emma, all of them looked like us, and suddenly I felt related to those children. I too began to talk about them as if it were only yesterday that somebody had come and taken them. I felt that a life had stopped, that an entire life was truncated forever, that a whole life to be filled with enormous happiness and a future remained sunken in anonymity—a life stolen.

I have spent all these weeks with René. I go to her house in the morning and we begin as I take a small recorder out of my bag and finish as I put it away, and I allow myself to be carried away by her words, by the darkness of her memory, by her silences, and by that which she denies recalling, and then I return to the hotel, where sleep will not come. I cannot understand how René has been able to live without knowing where her children are buried or if, perchance, they are still alive.

I told you that I came to write about the Mothers, but I do not know if my lexicon has run dry. Perhaps I will dedicate myself to only writing some poems, but it is now that I understand why I devote myself to the preservation of objects that perhaps do not exist. This is one of the characteristics of the displaced.

Magi

✳

January 1984

Dear Emma,

Very soon you will arrive in Santiago, and together we will tour our city, our streets where we knew what it meant to travel without surveillance, with a sense of security that only adolescence understands. We loved our Santiago, and we two lived in what they now call lower-class districts. But at that time, Nuñoa was the most noble area of the city. Do you remember how my father disliked living near Don Juan's butcher shop? But I enjoyed it because the flies and their incessant movements fascinated me. Many times I have felt as they: insignificant and mediocre before the immense constellations of our heavens. There is nothing I enjoy more and miss more than to look at the sky above Chile. I am certain that Gabriela Mistral in her imaginary paradise of Elquí also did that.

Yesterday I met with Violeta M. and the *arpilleristas*. This occurred in the usual place: the patio of the Vicariate. The winter sun and the distant fragrance of the lemon trees accompanied us. A chill ran through me as I saw them arrive with their frayed gloves, their faces and their coats of mourning, their tired shoes. They are women who have been frozen in a time of pain and perennial lamentation.

This reunion was much more fluid than the previous ones, and we truly enjoyed being together. They took out their fabric of lilacs and purples, full of life. They told me that it was more pleasant and easier to complete the appliqué in a group. I believe that it is this, this assemblage, that has given them the strength to re-create the families they have lost. You, most of all, remember what it used to signify to be the mother of a detainee or disappeared person in Chile. It was something akin to having leprosy. Everyone fled these mothers, saying, "I know nothing of the matter. [We don't] talk about that." But they, by means of their scraps of cloth, spoke indeed.

When I saw them together, readying the fabric, recounting what existed in the deepest recesses of their hearts, drinking a bit of lukewarm water with lemon peel, I drew near to them, for they represent the most beloved of Chile: the small towns and the people of the countryside, the humble folk. I say this without seeking superiority, but rather with the most heartfelt sincerity. That is my Chile, and I tell this to you as a Jew who has always felt a stranger to all these things and all these places.

The *arpilleristas* are luminous women, fine souls. The dictatorship has not been able to steal from them that angel of good spirits. I like to see them leaning over the cloth. Gently they thread the needle. They sigh. Sometimes they moan. Irma always creates an immense tree whose shade protects Jorge, who disappeared in 1973. Violeta always has numerous photographs of Newton Morales that she incorporates into *arpilleras* about Newton, who is seen as so full of life, overflowing the page. I like to feel their presence and caress these *arpilleras*.

I believe that we could help them. I do not refer so much to creating a small market for their *arpilleras* but instead to bringing about the propagation of their stories and making the lunacy and horror of all this known. I remember a phrase in the newspaper a few days ago that read: "Not a leaf moves in this country without my knowing it." I feel that the *arpilleras* are thousands of little leaves that, during the first moments of dawn, in the hands of enchantresses, recount the histories of our country, and Pinochet has not discovered them. Throughout the morning, the *arpilleras* are luminous leaves that cover the earth and say: "Where are they? Help us look for them."

My dear Emma, I do not know if I should be afraid for what we did yesterday in the Vicariate. After I left the meeting, a dark van without license plates followed me. It stopped in front of our house and stayed there for a long time. Very early in the morning it continued stalking me. I am worried, but not for my personal safety: they may involve my family. As you know, one of my cousins is married to an admirer of the military regime, and he has threatened my mother with informing on me. I, nonetheless, continue with my work as if it were the most natural thing in the world. Moreover, the reason I wish to continue this project has nothing to do with duty but instead with that essence of humanity that we should never lose: the solidarity, the willingness to extend a hand, to love one another and say, "I will give you hope."

I anxiously await your arrival. The city is not the same without you, dear Emma, because it is observed through a fear brought on by those men with ominous fangs pursuing us for being young and in love with life. Today I shall hear, thanks to the presence of our Violeta, some songs of the Chabuca Grande, and I am here in our beloved Latin America, so divine, so brutalized, but always our own.

I will meet you at the airport. A big kiss and may the angels accompany you.

Marjorie

September 1986
California

Dear Marjorie,

If only this moment had never come, or the reason for which I must write this letter. Some hours ago I received the telephone call that I never wanted to receive, and I was informed that my mother had died in Chile.

Her battle with cancer was long and painful, and my mother fought death, sword in hand, as her bitter enemy, for many years.

Tonight I am sad and I feel more alone than ever in this country so far from all that was mine. Memories come to mind—years, months, and moments that I want to capture in my memory so that they will remain as a permanent part of my present. For a few hours I wished I were a little girl again, pressing myself to my mother's bosom and breathing in that familiar scent of home-cooked food and lavender soap. I would like to hide my head in her embroidered apron and cry so that she could tell me, as she always did, that there is no pain in the life that does not pass. I want to open the book of my life to certain chapters and relive them again. I would like to change our histories, completely rewriting their endings. Why must we be so far from all those we love so much?

I feel so powerless, unable to change the course of time and cheat death with some excuse, although it be only for a few more years!

Marjorie, if I had not come to this country, so distant and so foreign, I could have spent thousands and thousands of days sharing moments of sorrow and joy with my mother's eternal smile. Life has been so fleeting that I have the horrible sensation of having been a child for only a few years, an adolescent for another few moments, and now am beginning to suddenly feel all the emptiness brought on by death without being prepared to become a woman, to be strong, to have matured into an invincible being. How will I live without that ever-present, certain voice that illuminated my decisions and loved me with an endless devotion during the good times and the bad?

Marjorie, you know that I have never understood the irrational conditions brought on by death, but now that it comes to me from afar and strikes me so closely, I understand less. But more than the incomprehensible irony of death, tonight I feel a devastating and impotent frustration faced with the inconsistent purpose of life. It seems as if my mother followed the uncertain road of this world with determination, bravely confronting her suffering without seeking to change her fate or choose a different life. She experienced the solitude of exile in a country that always felt painfully foreign to her, she tragically lost two children and loved with all her heart a man that emotionally and physically abused her throughout all the years of their marriage. After that Calvary, she then had to feel her body disintegrate from cancer, slowly, without the ability to fight, unable to use even that triumphant strength through which she had survived the constant tempests of her existence.

Perhaps because it is three o'clock in the morning, perhaps because I am wishing all this were only a nightmare from which I will awaken tomorrow, or perhaps because I want desperately to bring my mother back to this world, I feel tonight that life has less meaning than it had before. How can we fortify ourselves against this existence? What is the purpose of looking to the future, Marjorie?

It is late, late at night, and this night seems darker and colder than other nights. I hear in the distance the whistle of a train that passes through the center of the city, and the rhythm of that machine makes me think of how marvelous it would be to travel through space and time, to be transported to another place. On this night I would leave with unimaginable speed to sit on the edge of my mother's bed, and I would seal her eyes with a long kiss so that, finally, she would truly rest in her eternal sleep.

How little sense has the surprising arrival of death when we do not have those last precious minutes to say farewell to our fellow travelers. I have thousands of words that float through my mind tonight, so many things I want my mother to hear before she closes her eyes. But that monster, silent and dark, took her without granting me the final opportunity to tell her that each step I have taken since my first years of life has been guided by her unconditional and boundless love.

I want dawn to arrive, but at the same time I want this night to last forever so that tomorrow's light does not confront me, face-to-face, with the unmistakable truth of the death of my mother.

Write me, my friend.

Emma

❈

October 22, 1987
Reno, Nevada

My dear friend,

Last night at 7:10 P.M. my son Jonathan was born. After spending months in the hospital, suffering from the uncontrollable fear of losing my son or of falling asleep and never waking up, I finally saw his little body in my arms and opened my heart to life once again.

As you know, in these past few years, my feelings have swung between my fear of death and the powerful desire I have within me to struggle against it. Now as I gaze at the sweet, innocent face of my son, I feel new fears, new concerns invade me, but I assure myself that I am not going to die . . . I cannot die . . . I will [myself] not to die. My life begins again with the birth of my son.

I wanted to name him after my brother José Hugo, but I was afraid of reviving the tragic history of his predecessors. My mother attempted to defeat her superstitions and gave the same name to both my brothers. Both died in the same way. She wanted to challenge the forces of the unknown, but I prefer to accept them and not combat them.

Last night I thought about names for hours, hundreds of names that reminded me of people or events in our homeland. I recalled distant dreams, and considered giving him a name that would connect him to what remained hidden on the far side of our mountains. Marjorie, it might not seem important to others, but I wanted my son's name to sound like our names. I wanted to call him Rodrigo, Bernardo, Alejandro, or any other name in which I can hear the furor of the sea, the cavalcades in the countryside in springtime, or any sound that murmurs the uncontrollable "rr" of our language. I wanted to give him a name that, when spoken, would transport us to the world we left behind. But perhaps, most of all, I wanted to give him a name that, someday, would help him return to our memories, to our unfinished past, so that he, with renewed hopes, could exhume them.

All those names full of memories, heavy with the sounds of our language, were only infantile dreams. John reminded me that a Spanish name would be a disadvantage for our son in a country that does not tolerate the memories of its immigrants. Thus it has come to pass in the long history of my family that extends through Italy, Chile, Argentina, and the USA, that there was born, far from South America, a brown-skinned boy with dark eyes who was christened with an English name and an Irish surname: Jonathan Mulligan.

I have spent the entire day watching him sleep, reliving my past and thinking about what fate will bring him in this land, his land.

Will he identify with the customs of his father? Will he learn Spanish? Will I be able to teach him to love Chile as much as I do?

Through the window I see the trees, autumn-tinted, and I dream, I escape the sickly scent that drenches the drab walls of this hospital. My imagination carries me, and I watch my son grow, and a hopeful smile lights up my face. I see him taking his first steps, calling me "mami" (or will he call me MOM?). I imagine him asking me the names of the flowers, the color of my mother's eyes, or the distance from my heart to the sky. And then he becomes a man. I see him grown, discovering the secrets of love, and the passion for life, believing in my ideals, and wanting to save the world in a single lifetime. Will he see the world as I do? I don't know. I feel so much hope, alone this night in my adoptive city!!!

Marjorie, in a few months you will also hold a new life in your arms. Do you think it will be a boy or a girl? Have you thought of a name?

I hope our children continue our friendship and our histories, throughout the years and the continents, as we have done.

Take care and be patient — the final weeks are the worst, but when the day arrives, it will be one you'll never, ever forget.

Two big kisses (one from Jonathan).

Emma

❊

January 1988

Dear Emma,

I have longed to converse with you as we used to, back in a time when we would return after long vacations, were fearless in our adventures, and above all, were privileged to have unfettered hours and happiness granted by our leisure.

Good fortune, happiness, and plenitude have come to me again with the birth of Joseph Daniel, who bears the name of his great-grandfather Joseph Halpern . . . but without the spare time and the luxury of leisure. However, while this marvelous gift sleeps, I can write to you. Joseph saw the light of his first day on January 10, continuing a long tradition of family members born in the month of January, like his great-grandmother, grandmother, and uncle. The night before his birth here in New England, an enormous electrical storm erupted, the moon shone brightly, and icicles hung from the trees. Everything seemed an exquisite, sensual delight, an almost magical effervescence, but at the same time I felt that the night was not mine, that I was in the other hemisphere and did not know the names of the stars.

I had difficulty falling back asleep, but I decided to love the landscape left to me that earthly and celestial night. The following day, the sun glistened on a bright, golden blanket of snow. The contractions surged to their own rhythm, like fast and slow waves. I knew then that I had to continue the tradition of my race, and I invoked my women, my ancestors, so that they could help me in this infinite moment, an instance that is mine and belongs to all women, the moment of giving birth.

I have always loved that phrase, "to see the light," because it suggests everything that motherhood implies: the happiness of giving life, of making peace with all life, and of uniting oneself to the infinite human life of this Kingdom, giving us a true paradise on earth.

The delivery was painful and slow, but Joseph Daniel triumphed and came into the world jubilant, and full of joy and astonishment. John held him and kissed his little fingers. I believe that both of us experienced the most sublime and illuminating moment, as if for the first time we understood that we belonged to this dearly loved human family.

The births of Joseph and Jonathan make us think about the future of our children in this diaspora. What destiny will they forge in this country? What tales will they tell? I hope they learn about us, our legacy, and our passions. What stories will they tell in school? I hope they never experience what happened to us when we came to North America, when my teacher in Georgia told us that, because we were immigrants, we were fourth-class citizens . . .

I want *hispanidad* to be embraced as a cherished part of human life, of culture, of our dreams as well as the dreams of this America in which so often we are made invisible, this America that has tried to rob us of our identity by demanding we speak in English and only enjoy their homogeneous culture.

When I kiss Joseph, I coo lullabies that our mothers sang to us and whisper the verses of Gabriela Mistral. I want poetry to be part of his earliest memories. I want it to remain in his being and his imagination, but most of all I want him to love our language, the culture of which we are now part, and to comprehend that Chile, indeed, is the petal of a rose in bloom, as Neruda wrote.

Emma, I am certain that our children will play side-by-side, whether it be on the East Coast or the West Coast, and that they will come to love each other as we have.

Marjorie

✳

April 1989
Santiago, Chile

Dear Marjorie,

We have been in Chile for three days. We arrived at the moment in which the country is preparing for the elections that will decide if we continue the dictatorship or we return to a democracy. The favorite joke in the country is about the simple question that they ask on the plebiscite, "Yes or No?" They say that Pinochet believes the question is: No, they do not want me to leave or Yes, they want me to stay. But the truth is that the plebiscite is "yes" or "no" to retain the dictatorship. If the government loses, we will return to a democracy.

We have spent the entire day interviewing women of the Association of the Detained and Disappeared for our documentary. I believe that this has been one of my most difficult projects. Women who have lost their children, brothers and sisters, parents and husbands, tell us stories that you and I have heard so many times. But now when they retell them and I relive them in my memory, it is much more painful than before because I have to translate their stories in front of the cameras while they cry, and while I have a knot in my throat and tears run down my face. Often, I have to stop speaking so I can control my tears and begin again.

All the interviews have been painful, but some linger in my mind for hours after we finish filming. For example, the testimony of Doris, who does not want to leave Chile and be reunited with her family in Sweden because she is certain that someday she will find her son—who disappeared in 1973. This woman has lost her family because she will not give up her perpetual search for the answer to her question, the one asked by all these women: Where are they? These women live this constant agony minute by minute, day by day, and no one listens to them. Many have died over the years without knowing the fate of their loved ones, and others have lost part of themselves in the incessant search. Yesterday, while the women were seated in a circle talking about their experiences, a woman dressed in black approached, touched my shoulder, and gestured that she wanted me to follow her to a corner of the room where we were meeting. I stood and slowly followed her so as not to interrupt the conversation of the group. In the corner, the woman opened her old handbag and gave me a small booklet of poems illustrated with the photo of a baby on the cover. I took it and asked her whose it was and who was the person on the cover. The woman only looked me in the eyes without saying a single word. I asked her the same questions again, and this time she took my hand and pressed it between her own, and then kissed my hand without saying a thing. I was enormously moved by her expression, but at the same time I was exasperated that she would not say a word, so I gripped her by the shoulders and shook her body impatiently, repeating: "Talk to me, tell me something, please, I want to know who you are and whose book this is." The woman made no sound, she only embraced me tightly, and when our bodies were pressed together, I heard the succession of desperate sobs that sprang from her throat. We spent some time embracing each other until other women stood up from the circle and came to talk to me. They explained that Mercedes, the woman who was hugging me, had written the book, and the baby in the photo was her only son. The soldiers detained him when he was eighteen years old and beat him in her presence, then carried him away from their home. Mercedes never saw her son again. Slowly she became enveloped in silence and never spoke again. Now she only writes, and she carries photos of her son when he was a baby — but not any photos that are of him when he was older, or from the time when they detained him. Mercedes lives alone, writing and sewing onto her *arpilleras* the memories that she carries within her of her son, but only those memories of when he was less than a year old. I spoke with her for a few moments and, although she followed my words with rapt attention and occasionally nodded her head as a sign of agreement, not a single sound left her mouth. After speaking with Mercedes, I felt the pain of all those absences, those disappearances, and those profound wounds that will never heal . . . they came to me in a torrent and toppled me, there, in front of all those tremendously heroic, extremely stoic women. I was unable to stay there for the rest of the interviews — I said good-bye to the women and informed the director that I was returning to the hotel.

I left the Vicariate and found myself facing the immense building of the Cathedral of Santiago, the house of God, as the nuns told me so many times in Our Savior Preparatory, my unforgettable school where I was taught to pray. I walked to the main entrance of the cathedral and climbed the stairways covered with paralyzed, blind, and hungry beggars that shook the coins in their alms jars. I passed among those faces of human misery and entered through the huge wooden doors toward the interior of the church, I walked directly to the altar and knelt before all those images that had protected me for so many years during my childhood, and instead of praying I began to cry. I do not know how long I wept, Marjorie, but finally I felt a great sensation of relief and tranquility. I believe that those were the tears that I had carried inside of me since I left this country and went there, to the North, far from my people and my paths, tears that I had been unable to shed. Chile needs our tears so that the people will awaken instead of remaining in this slumber caused by the terror of the dictatorship, a regime that has already lasted too many years and has swallowed up too many of the dead.

Dear Marjorie, how I wish you were here with me now so that we could walk together, treading upon the dry leaves in Forest Park to the bank of the Mapocho River. We could talk about so many things and remember these women, these women who cannot cease dreaming about the spring that will return democracy to our homeland again. As it was so many years ago when September arrived, bringing with it the presidential election, the flowers, and on the eighteenth the birthday of our homeland. Do you remember those Septembers? I recall so many things now from my small room of the Foresta Hotel.

Tomorrow should be a better day in this painful project. The director told me that the name of the movie will be *Threads of Hope*. They plan to travel to Wellesley to interview you immediately after they return to Canada. Meanwhile, rest and take good care of Joseph.

Love,
Emma

❋

May 7, 1990

Dearest Emma,

I am certain that you remember the misnamed Colonia Dignidad from when you were little. What was a small hostel/hotel is now a concentration camp on the curving paths of southern Chile. Uncertain travelers, innocent tourists pause in the lobby to savor the Austrian cuisine and the strudels. Everything was much too delicate, Emma, and the order was harmonious. Everything was rigid and dangerously civilized. The few times that I traveled to the south I was moved by the transparency of certain women selling dried meat or those that seemed to be dressed in the first rainfall, the agile dew, and time seemed to hesitate before the schedule of routes and forebodings such as the flight of birds or the course of certain stars through the limpid, uninhabited, cloudless sky.

Today we know so much about Colonia Dignidad as well as about our homeland. Emma, what happened to us during all these unwonted years? How has it been possible to have lived years of disquieting solidarity? How did we prepare ourselves to leave behind our summers at the magnificent beaches of Zapallar where they accept neither Arabs nor Jews, but they teach the peasants to read? Our solidarity made us share a drink at the movie theater as well as our salary with the needy. We were a blissful country. The elections took place amid balloons and taciturn clowns. We never were a country that irradiated happiness. On the contrary, a certain sadness pleased us, a certain pain in being a poor and despised country in the face of the colossal Argentina. But now I ask: what happened to us? How did that solidarity vanish and how did we go from being a people of kind folk and friendly neighbors to informers? All this I ask you now while we listen to the darkest news: news that we had already suspected and that was rumored in secret meetings. Colonia Dignidad was indeed a torture center and a place where they raped little girls and took their lives at the tender age of ten years. We know that 122 missing persons were found alive, but, Emma, they are as dead, imprisoned by a harrowing thirst brought on by the complicity of the other corpses pressing upon their bodies.

Where do we belong, dear Emma, within the amnesia of our homeland, in the face of comfort, before the forgetfulness, confronted by the negation of life and memory? As you know, the Jews live obsessed with preserving memory because a people that forgets is a people without past or future. Don't you think that is true? Sometimes I think that throughout the night the voices of the disappeared moan and ask us to remember them. Is that not immortality?

Magi

December 14, 1990

Dear Emma,

I imagine that you are already in your house in Reno, surrounded by all your beloved objects: your photographs of our America through which you have traveled minutely in all its diminutive magnificence so that you could fix it within your invented, inventive memory; so you could feel it inside you, so that they no longer tell you that you are a foreigner, a stranger in all places. Perhaps you walked through hills and valleys, you crossed rivers, and you photographed all the women of our continent who pass unnoticed and are very tenacious in the zones of forgetfulness. Memory is an exercise rarely desired in this weak homeland full of fears.

But today I am writing you from Isla Negra—after more than sixteen years, I have finally returned to this village of my coast. You will recall that my family and I would spend our summers in Quisco and that, in the afternoons when the sun seemed an enormous dome with tresses of red and orange, my mother and I would walk arm-in-arm with our fingers entwined, bound for the island to see if, there, the poet was out for a walk with one of his huge notebooks and his pens of green ink. I enjoyed the pleasure of being with my mother alone and talking about the harmony of the universe. Once she handed me some stones. She made me look to the sky and then touch the water with my bare feet. She told me: "You are rich with the wealth of the universe." That moment, Emma, stayed with me and has helped me through moments of hopelessness and solitude. It is a daily messenger of happiness.

Today I have returned to Isla Negra to once more feel that I conserve the gratitude of the universe within my arms and that I am here, that I have survived. Everything flourishes in Isla Negra. The home of Neruda, that before had some enormous signs announcing that the house was closed, is now open to the public and is crowded with scholars and cheerful voices. It is now a house that lives and sings.

I wander through his house that, for the first time, seems to be truly mine. I find that Chile has entered into me through my soul, through my pores, through each of my veins, until I finally feel that I am the one displaced, and through this house I enter the histories of murders, horrors, and arrests that have not been in vain because the people, the humble as well as the most powerful and arrogant, come to this house and are imbued with a common happiness upon seeing the figureheads bearing names of languid women and knowing that his poetry is alive, and that Matilde and Pablo greet us from their tombs, receiving all their guests, always welcome and never inopportune.

It will take many years to discover what really happened in our homeland. What was it that could transform such a peaceful and civil country into a place where neighbors denounced one another and whole families did not speak to each other for decades? Were we always so, a country condemned to fascism, a country that hated foreigners, one unsettled by the scarce presence of the Jews? Or did we suddenly become another people, and the memories of our nation were no longer our own? In order to survive we chose amnesia, we pretended we were strangers, we repeated "I know nothing about the matter" when our young people disappeared, while in the classroom the teacher remained impassive and continued with the lesson.

I walk along this rocky coast as I did when I was a child, and I recognize each of these rocks, each one of these precipices and narrow passes. I sit down and the sea sits next to me like a shared horizon, a long extension of happiness, endless. I lean, unhurried, and I anoint my lips in the sea. I smile and remember my mother, who was always right: in my hands and in my skin I have the whole universe.

We believe that peace has finally returned to this island. Democracy has also returned to this Chile, this nation that I have always loved, which now returns to me like a puzzle box that is opened one layer at a time, like someone who awakens before the first buds in the garden of spring.

Love you more than ever,
Marjorie

✳

December 1991
Costa Brava, Chile

Dear Marjorie,

I am experiencing an immense and incomparable happiness. The Chilean soil is once again beneath my feet and, after so many years, it is a land that is clean and free. One has yet to see the changes brought on by democracy, but there are clear indications that the dictatorship no longer reigns in the streets nor in the air of our cities. The machine guns have disappeared from the hands of the police, and soldiers walk cautiously en route to their barracks. The press has been freed from the control of censorship and people once again pause at the kiosks to read the headlines of the daily newspapers, with a smile on their lips. But amid this new atmosphere still exists that sadness which marks our entire people as they walk from corner to corner, with their vivid memories and the tragedy still burning in their hearts. It seems that silence has been encrusted in the routine of the people. Nobody wishes to say anything about the new government, nobody has an opinion, nobody criticizes, all obey the command of silence because, deep down, people fear that after so many years of dictatorship this is only a distant mirage, the illusion of a lake of clear water in the middle of the desert.

I have spent most of my time in this little house in Costa Brava, on the edge of the sea. As you will remember, our house is a true refuge, an escape from the winters in Nevada and the hectic and demanding life in the USA, as well as the limiting and obligatory tasks that never leave me enough time to write. Here in this paradise of white houses, sand, sun, and the fresh scent of the sea, I can write until dawn without ever realizing what time it is. Afterward, in the mornings when the sun rises, I get up and walk along the seashore between the gulls and rocks that border the beaches. Sometimes I walk to Con Cón, where the fishermen's small boats arrive with their daily catch of fish and shellfish, selling to shoppers who hope to find the best and freshest delicacies of the eastern rim of the Pacific. I observe the simple and unfettered world of the fishermen, and I sit for long periods dreaming about what my life would have been like if I had never left this land, if I had stayed to live forever on the shore of this sea. Life on this side of the world seems truer, simpler, and purer. My world in the USA is always devoured by the metallic tangle of inhuman highways, of people who run throughout the night and slumber during the day, hoping to make their way through the insensitive forces of a capitalism that devours and consumes, consumes and devours. I as yet do not know if my spirit will survive the annihilating machinery of that America. I am aware that we cannot return to the paths we left behind, and I no longer feel the necessity of returning, but I do want, somehow, to never forget this simple and fulfilling way of life.

Here, surrounded by the perpetual silence of my people, in my country numbed by the pain of these seventeen years, I have finished the final corrections on my book *We, Chile: Testimonies of the Chilean Arpilleristas*. I am not certain if it was the sea, or the tears of the women who told me their stories, or simply the interminable power of a silence that I have never learned to love, but two nights ago I continued writing until three in the morning and completed the pages of the manuscript.

I miss you very much, and Chile also. I have become accustomed to hearing the echo of your laughter during our strolls along Valparaiso Street and our long conversations at a table outside the Samoyedo Cafe in Viña del Mar.

I hope to see you in Mexico in April.

Best wishes,
Emma

✳

January 1993

Dearest Emma,

There are so many things I wish to write to you about, and
also so much I want to find out about you, about your beautiful
son who is growing up in this country that now both is, and is not,
ours. I also want to tell you about that which has united us and
has been a constant part of our dialogue: Chile, that small, golden,
luminous fringe of South America that makes us weep from rage
and overpowering emotions. Exile has brought us privileges, such
as the possibility of articulating, being, feeling the language that
we stopped speaking. Many times I review certain words as if I
were dealing with ancient books in Yiddish. Sometimes I call you
to speak in Chilean and laugh in Chilean, to experience the rich-
ness of speech that can only be felt among people who belong to
certain places. But I also question that. Belonging to a landed aristocracy permitted you to enjoy certain privileges but denied you
others. You could not go to a mixed school, you could not go out
with Jews. Above all, you had to always be a young lady sitting
with your knees together, with perfect posture. My privilege was
in not belonging, or rather, being a daughter of the first Jewish
professor in a school of medicine, which marked me profoundly
but, at the same time, permitted me numerous freedoms, since in
the eyes of those of your social class we were barefoot beggars
without a homeland. Now we two are without a homeland and
when we return they punish us—the punishment may be the look
other professionals give us because of our success or our academic
situation that permits us a certain prosperity. The punishment
manifests itself in very subtle turns of the language, such as, for
example, "Certainly you can, because you left . . ." or "Of course,
in contrast to you, *we* Chileans . . ." What are we, Emma, parallel
beings? And what are we in this supposed multicultural amalgam
that is our America?

I only ask you all these things because I believe that perhaps your destiny and mine have become this perpetual condition of foreignness within and outside of our country, but it is more painful for us when it comes from that Chile that we so zealously defended and fought for from a distance, that Chile in which we grew up as part of a generation. I remember how we two, during our vacations, fought for and participated in community activities, such as traveling to the south to teach the poor townspeople to read. Now one could say that those of our generation projected their ideals, that they did not fear the working class, because all this was part of what we called our homeland.

The years of dictatorship have converted us into a nation fearful of ourselves and of community action. We had to exist, defending the doubtful peace of the family while knowing that certain sectors of the capital suffered the most dire poverty, and that little girls were prostituted for a piece of bread.

I remember that during the saddest period of the Popular Unity, people had already intuited their defeat. In those times of absolute shortage, my cousin boasted of having enough water to water his golf course. In which zone did we live? On whose side did we place ourselves? Because everything had its time, its space, and its perverse ownership. Perhaps, Emma, that was the Chile that had always existed and we sensed that, wishing it were not so.

My return makes me think that perhaps we were and will be a country of traitors. The disastrous intervention of the CIA also involved us in the constant treason of that America of the North, the other America that was perplexed by the victory of the Popular Unity and decided to defeat us and continue with their legacy as cannibals and traitors. In a recent university conference of the supposed Chilean intelligentsia, the discussion became a savage critique devoid of all humanity. Some fascist teachers of the Catholic University criticized me publicly. They abstained at first from participating in an anthology because it was published in the United States, but afterward it was they themselves who became noted everywhere and in all the newspapers of the capital.

Painful is our homeland, Emma, but loved by us as well because, perhaps, our Chile is not found in the faces of the powerful or in the treacherous countenance of General Pinochet, but rather in the happy child with his one balloon on a Sunday outing or in the eyes of a miner, proudly watching his son receive a degree in medicine. This is the Chile that you and I love.

I hope you are well and take care of your son.

I love you,
Marjorie

＊

January 1993
Costa Brava, Chile

My dear compatriot,

I received your last letter before leaving for Chile, and I was deeply touched. For several days, since I arrived in our beloved Chile, I have been thinking of the same conflicts that you mentioned.

I accept that exile has given us privileges, but they are not unlike those we would have had in our country. We were both on our way to completing an excellent, "privileged" education. And you know that, sooner or later, we would have done something "memorable" and "revolutionary" with our lives. Marjorie, we have invincible spirits and we will always keep our dreams alive. For years, you have worked in defense of human rights, and your writing has opened the eyes of thousands of people that otherwise would never have understood the torture of children, mothers, and men—all tortured because they sought a better future for their homeland.

As I walk the streets of Santiago, the same streets that were filled with trucks loaded with soldiers, I wonder if you and I could have survived the dictatorship in silence, without risking our lives to save other lives. Marjorie, the country has suffered, and has survived, but is now like another world. It is no longer the country in which we grew up, it is a country that belongs to those who have reinvented it, and for us there is no space, only our memories of better days when we experienced the small victories of a so-called democracy. We can no longer go back. Nor can we change this country where the rich deny there was any torture and the poor die from hunger and despair.

I understand that we are no longer from here, nor are we from there, but somehow we must continue fighting for a better world, one much farther away. And now follows a news flash that is quite in keeping with our philosophical discussion . . .

I am seriously considering running for office in the 1994 elections in Nevada. I cannot stay on the sidelines, do nothing or only react to what happens in U.S. politics. This country, in spite of all its problems (as we have long discussed), has given me special opportunities, and the moment has come for me to serve in a public office, to try to give something back to my adoptive homeland, and to try to make changes for the better. I know that this news is going to utterly shock you, because you abhor politics and think it's a dirty game, but you'll have to remember that politics is in my blood and I feel, very deeply feel, that my moment has arrived.

I'll give you a few days to digest the news, then I'll call you so you can help me make my final decision.

Emma

October 21, 1993

Dearest Marjorie,

Today was my son JJ's sixth birthday. When he got out of bed this morning he asked if Grandpapa Hugo was going to call him from Chile to tell him happy birthday. I assured him that, yes, of course, his grandfather would never forget his grandson's birthday. He accepted that but didn't stop peppering me with questions. He always wants to know more. How much land does Grandpapa have? Why does he kill birds with his shotgun? Why did they write his name in blue paint on the streets near his house? JJ's questions have always been difficult to answer, but today it was nearly impossible to respond without revealing the profound sadness I felt as he questioned me. As you know, my father died two days ago, but we still haven't told JJ the truth.

My father's death was the fourth of the six members of my family, and I find that fact depressing and hard to accept. After he lost the mayoral elections, his health deteriorated and in a few months his cancer mercilessly overtook him. I spoke with him on the phone on numerous occasions, but I was never able to forgive him, something he had hoped to hear. I couldn't manage to forget the past and erase the memories of the life my father had forced us to endure. This brilliant man with a wonderful family, blessed with success and prosperity, could not control himself and live a normal life. In politics, he was passionate and willing to give his all for others. His enormous generosity made him help anyone that needed his unconditional support. He was always prepared to devote himself to others, but never to his own family, those who truly needed him. My father led a double life. As a public figure, he was admired by all, but he also had a private life that I never understood and always hated. Now he is dead, Marjorie, and his death hurts me, but not in the same way as when, years ago, I lost my brother and mother.

My father's death makes me sad because all death is unpleasant. But I am also confused by his death . . . it has unearthed tears that I shed so many years ago, tears that he could have stopped, but instead he did nothing. He could have changed, but he didn't. He should have loved us in another way, but he couldn't. He could have been a true father, but he wasn't. And so, tonight, I should be shedding the tears that, perhaps, he deserves, but I can't. Nevertheless, as I write to you, I am crying, but they are tears of pain and anger. Pain because it is too late, and anger because he died without undoing the harm that he caused.

Tonight, when I put JJ to bed, he kept asking me about his grandfather. He wasn't able to understand why Grandpapa hadn't called him today. Although I wanted to protect him, to save him from suffering the loss of his beloved grandfather, I told my son the truth. I sat on the edge of his bed and turned on the light. I held his little hands, looked in his eyes, and said, "Grandpapa Hugo didn't call you because he is dead." JJ immediately responded with another question: "When did he die, Mami?" I told him and he remained calm, accepting death as he would have any other story. He didn't cry or become sad. Instead, JJ only added that he was going to love him the same whether he was alive or dead.

Perhaps tonight I am writing you because I need to put these feelings down on paper, to get them out of me, and they make me think about a faraway and peaceful forgiveness that will slowly fill me as the days pass. Because I finally took the first step, maybe too late, but I did it. The last time I spoke to my father, I wrote him a long letter after I hung up the phone, and I told him how terrible my life had been with him, and how I wanted him to realize that before he died and, although he might not understand why, I wanted to forgive him. Early the next morning the phone rang, and it was his new wife informing me that my father had died at dawn. Since there is a five-hour time difference between Chile and Nevada, maybe he closed his eyes at the moment I was writing that letter of forgiveness. I never sent the letter, but surely my father's spirit read it before departing this world.

Marjorie, my friend, I am writing you tonight, like on so many other sad nights. My father died, my son loved him and continues to love him even after his death, and I am struggling with my anguish and a desperate desire to forgive . . . but I cannot find the path that leads me to peace, to truly forgiving and forgetting.

Kisses,
Emma

November 1994
Reno, Nevada

My dear friend Marjorie,

It is two o'clock in the morning and I am seated in front of a window through which I can see the pale moonlight that illuminates the sad skies of Nevada.

Across the miles, you experienced it with me, this year of endless and exhausting walks through the neighborhoods in my district, going house to house, speaking with young people, workers, housewives, professionals, the elderly who live on fixed incomes, and the interminable number of my Latino brothers and sisters who have no rights in this city.

Marjorie, this has been one of the most enriching experiences of my life. The problems I confronted and the stories I heard have opened my eyes, and I have witnessed the subcultures that exist in the margins of this rich and admirable country. I entered the homes of elderly people who lived alone and each day had to decide whether to buy food or medicine. I visited the homes of hardworking Latinos who held two jobs but couldn't afford medical coverage for their children. I spoke with women who home-schooled their children because they did not have faith in public education. I met people in favor of capital punishment and against abortion. People who wanted to build more prisons and fewer schools. I saw and I learned so much. I could have fought for changes and given a voice to those who go unheard.

Tonight, as the final results were announced, I felt a terrible pang of sadness and impotence. I was saddened by the loss of an opportunity to use my experience in politics and frustrated to see that so many people are uninterested in working toward solutions; they consider themselves beaten and don't vote. In my district there are more than 60,000 people, only 29,000 are registered voters, my opponent won with about 8,000 votes, and I lost with almost 6,000. Another few votes went to the Libertarians, and so this election was decided by the minority, like so many other elections in the USA in 1994.

The Republican Party, as they had repeatedly promised with their lamentable "Contract with America," took the reins of the country, not only in Congress but in many other elections.

I am overwhelmed with contradictory feelings on this sad winter night. I do not know if it is the last night I will dream about creating changes through the power of politics, or if it is the first night of my disenchantment with the political game.

Also tonight, sitting in front of this desk that has seen me cry thousands of times, from both happiness and pain, I feel great pride in knowing that I am one small dreamer, defending the rights of the less fortunate, a combatant without rest, and I, after so many years in [my] adopted country, have managed to be the first Latina immigrant to represent the Democratic Party in a senate race in the state of Nevada.

But also, my dear and old friend, I feel an unmeasurable sadness because the democracy of this country is for sale. The elections belong to whoever amasses the most money, and the businesses buy the candidates at a good price.

How terrible that in this country, where there is so much, it all seems to be destined for the few. People talk about better education for their children, raising the minimum wage, rights for minorities and women, social security, and a better system of health care. But almost nobody votes. They complain about an entity called "the government," they attack its laws and the power that "the government" supposedly has, but when there are opportunities for change, they all sit on the sidelines and do absolutely nothing.

Perhaps you were right when you told me that we could achieve some things in this country but, when it comes right down to it, we will always be immigrants and never a part of the machinations of power in this land.

Before I started this letter, I read several pages of the personal diary that I kept during the campaign. Marjorie, writing has saved us many times. Now as I read it again, I realize how awful a political campaign can become. I still can't believe that my opponents obtained my medical records and discovered I had lupus — and that they published the information in the newspaper! Doesn't a person with a chronic illness have the right to enter politics? Do you remember when that reporter called me to confirm that my son went to school in another country? Or the reporter who said that my conservative father was a communist? It all now seems like a long nightmare. But we woke up, my friend, and I am once again free. After tonight, no more threats, attacks, or lies.

In a few days I return to my students and my academic world.

And to my writing. Who knows . . . perhaps even a book about the campaign.

I'll call you tomorrow so you can help me get through this.

Thank you for helping me to dream this dream. Don't you dare think that it will be my last.

Now let's reelect Bill Clinton. He's our only hope.

Your friend who lost the battle but not the war.

All my love,
Emma

P.S. Do I have to refund your campaign contribution? After all, you were buying access. Weren't you?

✳

June 1995

My unforgettable Emma,

I am writing you during this summer of heavy rain. It has been a long time since I have seen it rain like this in New England, where our hands have become accustomed to the land and where I sometimes dream about the voracity of our mountain ranges. The rain creates the opportunity to meditate. I remember the words of Thomas Merton where he talks about certain rainfalls, like those in the city, and that one does not resemble another, and the rain in the desert is a festival of gratitude. This is how I feel, Emma, while I write you with enormous gratitude, knowing that you are close by.

Today they have granted me full professorship at Wellesley, considered one of the best universities in the country and not just a university of daughters of the well-to-do, as the envious usually say. Obviously it is a place for certain people of privilege. But it is not the fleeting privilege of the nouveau riche; rather it refers to that privilege that has to do with being chosen, of being born with all rights. That is to say, here have been educated the daughters of some dictators, among them Somoza and Madame Chiang Kai-shek, as well as extraordinary women like Madeleine Albright and Hillary Clinton, women that now are pivotal in North American politics. I wonder about my place in this university that, on one hand, has given me opportunities and privilege, forms of being and of not being, giving me freedom, but, on the other hand, their administration, that is to say their bureaucracy, constantly accuses me of not being one of them, of not conforming to the petty rituals that form part of those who belong in the colleges and North American academe. Which means, formerly I did not sit down and partake in languid teatimes at dusk and talk about espadrille shoes and cultured pearls. Nor today do I meet for the hollow dialogues that they have about genre and multiculturalism because this college represents extraordinary privilege within these changes: it can be permitted the luxury of diversity, a luxury that, here, is empty rhetoric. The proof lies in that in a college like Wellesley there are practically no Hispanic professors and few African Americans. I recall the celebrated words of my friend, the writer from Ghana, Ama Ata Aido, and I quote her because she has given me permission to do so. She asked me: "How is it possible that we are eating in this splendid club and I am the only black woman in the place?"

The day of my full professorship, I noticed that my father was deeply moved, almost crying. You know him, he is a man of great modesty, but I was able to glimpse in his look a mixture of nostalgia and sadness. I felt that he was considering me and our shared achievements. He told me: "Who would have thought that the granddaughter of a Russian Jewish tailor working from beneath an umbrella would someday come to be a university professor?" All this makes me question so many things. Our place in society causes us to be perennial foreigners in the space of academe. It also makes me think about the space we occupy as Latinas.

I have been happy at Wellesley, Emma, alongside great friends, magical women, guides and mentors. Among them is Elena, who has had a great influence in our lives. But in spite of the fact that I teach at Wellesley, I am not exactly from here, and there is something in these walls that makes me think of strange times when foreigners such as I do not belong and where they look at us

with a mixture of exoticism and perverse curiosity. I have been
happy sharing my passion for human rights and the literature of
our women with the Northern Hemisphere, and I have been able
to unite passions. However, in the social functions I am viewed
with disdain. They do not get too close to me, fearing that my truth
is not like their own, and they are suspicious. I cannot stop thinking about the experiences of my father when he began in academe — experiences that always made him feel left out at the parties
and meetings, especially since he was one of the most prominent
and prolific professors but had one of the lowest salaries in the
country.

North American academia is like a corporation in this country,
and I am giving you my sincerest opinion colored by a great degree of prejudice and even anger. We do not realize that this
democracy functions through the aggressive imposition of rigid
canons, and so here we are, coming from a culture that promotes
passion and then invalidates it, in a society that denies it under the
guise of intellectuality and objectivity. However, we are here,
Emma, having left behind the disastrous dictatorships of our
homeland and trying to build a space of our own.

I think that, even with all its conflicts, Wellesley has occupied
an essential place in my life because at least I am in a women's college whose fundamental mission is to teach women and permit
them to have success at all the levels, but more than anything to
empower them.

My dear Emma, we are now professional women, but I still
feel very alone, like a woman who writes and is not afraid of using
words and of speaking with her hands, although in Wellesley this
is not considered in good taste.

Magi

October 1995

Dear Emma,

We just returned from Miami where we celebrated the Letras de Oro awards. I was accompanied by my parents, my brothers and sisters, and our children. Together we celebrated something that means so much to our Hispanic culture. It is very impressive knowing that they recognize the efforts and talents of our community of Spanish-speaking writers. I say "community" because I feel completely and absolutely a part of this group that writes in Spanish. It is paradoxical that we would be surprised by our own existence, but you must remember that in Arizona, New Mexico, and Florida, Spanish was spoken long before the nineteenth century. We both understand that language is identity, culture, the ability to define oneself, to feel and to be. I am glad I kept our language alive, with its warm, passionate textures and its delicate shades of dark and light.

Dear Emma, the Letras de Oro awards, although quite renowned, did not have the elegance I would have liked. I am not referring to trivial refinements, but instead to real, elementary things that would give it a certain beauty. For example, I believe we should have celebrated with wineglasses made of crystal and not plastic, don't you agree? In short, I believe that if a woman had been in charge of the details, it would have been a different event, very different. There was something lacking in what should be a memorable event: a flower or perhaps a welcoming smile. But did you notice . . . as I raised my glass of champagne, I winked at you.

When I finished writing that book I was very afraid. I thought no one would publish it. Look, Emma, at how happy I am for winning a prize. I am certain that Van Gogh, wherever he may be, is watching me, and is happy about the union between poetry and painting, word and image.

I love you very, very much, my dearest friend.

Magi

AMIGAS

※

November 1996
Reno, Nevada

Dear friend,

After speaking with you on the phone, JJ and I left the house. I dropped him off at John's office, continued on my way, and a few minutes later, a woman didn't stop for a red light and ran into me. I was terrified as I watched her big car coming right at me and feeling that my life could end in a matter of seconds. When I regained consciousness, some people had opened my door and were asking if I was injured. My head hurt, and so did my nose and my right leg all the way up to my hip. I immediately remembered John's phone number and someone called him. A few minutes later, lights flashing and sirens wailing, the ambulance came on the scene. At the moment they were carrying me on the stretcher with my neck in a brace, I saw JJ as he got out of his father's car, his eyes wide with fear. I wanted them to lower the stretcher, to run and hug him, but I couldn't—so I gave him a thumbs-up, indicating that I was all right. JJ raised his little fist and made the same gesture and, silently, we both knew that we would be fine.

With your extrasensory powers, you should have realized that you needed to keep me on the phone a few minutes more so that the woman would have missed me!

I am doing well in spite of everything. They had to operate on my nose, and I have to have physical therapy to rehabilitate my knee and hip. The blow to my skull was so severe that they have to wait a few days to operate, when I'm better. Looking at the calendar, I realize that I have been spared having to cook a turkey and bake apple pies, two things that one must do to be the perfect American wife.

I have received so many flowers that my bedroom, as well as the rest of my house, has been transformed into the Garden of Eden. You are right, I have more friends than enemies in this city.

Please don't add to the tons of flowers that I already have around me . . . send me some Chilean *empanadas* and write me soon.

A big kiss,
Emma

July 1997

Dear Emma,

I have returned to Chile this winter, invited by the Ministry of Education to participate in the celebration of the centennial of "our Gabriela" (that is what we learned to call her in school, do you remember?). On rare occasions you spoke to me of her, and I wonder if in your journeys through La Serena you did not find out anything about her. Do you remember that from Elquí I traveled to Norte Chico and participated in her classes on education? So many times I have wondered about her solitude, and I sometimes believe that she felt more alone in Chile than outside of it. Her ideas did not sit well with those of the petit bourgeoisie with whom she found herself involved. Nothing, yet deep down everything, belonged to her. But I am writing to you about Gabriela because it is through her that I am meditating about what Chile is: a complex nation almost lost between the mountain range and the sea, a country of men dressed in gray and the silent dead walking behind them.

I decided to go to the General Cemetery. Other times I have been accompanied by Violeta Morales, but now I wish to go alone. I arrived at the gate and purchased bouquets of lilacs and violets. I remembered that old song that my mother used to sing to me, "Do you want flowers, Miss?" Do you remember it? Or that other song that our mothers sang, "Poppies"? We are getting old, Emma of my heart. All this is a way of connecting with a usurped past that no longer belongs to us.

As I entered the cemetery I saw the monument to the disappeared and the executed political prisoners. I could not stop the

rush of emotion, the feelings of rage and fear, and I thought, how 157
could we have lived so many years with so many lies and with so
much anger? I paused and read all the names. I recognized some
of them, including those from the Jewish community. Two were
classmates of me and my sister. I do not know what to tell you. I
read their names and prayed for them with the words of the old
Jewish prayer that is called Kaddish. I like to be seated next to
that monument, so simple and so noble, built with the money of
their relatives who are mostly unknown female victims of the
oppression.

Do you recall that on the day it was unveiled, not a single
member of our new and supposedly democratic government attended? Nobody wanted to be seen alongside the names of a magnificent and noble generation. The view from the cemetery makes
me think about what Chile is and, also, what occurs in these supposed democracies filled with fear and treason. So I feel myself
this morning sunk in a profound sadness, full of doubts about this
homeland that saw us grow and gave us words, but also gave us
silence.

I believe that, more than just being a cemetery, it is here,
where the dead reside, that we can discover so many things about
the history of our country, here, next to the monument to the disappeared. I come to this sacred and beautiful place, the park of
memories, and I find myself in front of the tomb of Salvador Allende, always covered with fresh flowers and messages of love.
The inscription surrounding it says: "From history are people created." Do you believe that we, in some way, have also managed to
build our own history in exile, to give voice to all the Violetas?
Next to the tomb of Allende is that of Jorge Guzmán, who was
murdered on the patio of the Catholic University, which today is
sponsoring the program on Gabriela Mistral. This is our homeland, my dear Emma, an experience vis-à-vis Salvador Allende
and Jorge Guzmán. One was the socialist president of our generation, the president that we loved, the president that represented a
challenge to injustice, and the other Jorge Guzmán, the creator of
the regime of Pinochet.

Magi

✳

My dear friend,

When you left this morning on the ship from Miami, you and your John, and sailed toward the deep oceans to the north, I felt enormously happy, remembering our lives and our experiences, experiences we had never dreamed of having. I remained there a long while, in silence, holding the hand of my John, this man that anchors my life with a strength and determination that only he possesses. I thought about how time has added new links to our chain of descriptive words, how we have been transformed into beings so different than we were before. Now we are wives, mothers, writers, teachers, exiles, and eternal immigrants in a divided land. What can be the meaning of all this?

Tonight, while looking at the sea from Miami, I wanted to write you and tell you how marvelous it was to receive the GEMS Television award for "Woman of the Year in Literature." It was wonderful because you were with me. The image of your John and my John, seated in that audience of strangers, brought to mind memories irreconcilable with our current existence. While I spoke at the microphone and wept, I saw your face in the crowd, looking up at me from between our gray-haired, gringo husbands. Marjorie, so many of our beautiful dreams have become a reality, but we have also suffered beyond our wildest dreams. In those moments, in front of all those people, I wanted to leave the stage, take you by the hand, and run in search of our unfinished past waiting somewhere between the mountains and the sea. But the second I saw you beside the tear-filled eyes of my John, I understood that perhaps I had to accept this world now, and not the one that we left behind, for this is the one that marks our destiny.

Dear friend, little by little I am realizing we are no longer from there, but I feel that neither are we from here. Will it be that we will never completely belong anywhere?

AMIGAS

What an honor it was to receive that prize! The words I spoke last night onstage still echo in my ears: "May this prize be a small homage to the memory of my mother that rests forever in the distant land of my birth, Chile." How I would have liked to find her smile among those strange faces. How happy my mother would have felt upon seeing that her rebellious little girl has found her way in the world and has dedicated her life to so many causes. Does she know, wherever she may be, that she still inspires me in everything I do, I write, and I say? Do you think she knows, when I would lose a battle, that she was the standard that rose before me and gave me the courage to stand and fight?

Next week, the awards ceremony will be broadcast in Latin America. In Chile, my classmates will see it, each now married with twenty children. The few college friends who survived the dictatorship will also see it. So will the hundreds of members of my Italian-Argentine family on the other side of the Andes. In every corner of South America it will be seen. . . . Will some of them recognize my smile? Will they be glad to see me again? I don't know, my friend. A lot of water has passed under those bridges—I can't believe that more than thirty years have passed.

I hope you enjoy your trip in the Caribbean.

I'll see you in Chile in December.

My love always,
Emma

❋

January 1998

Dear Emma,

At this moment, as I feel myself trapped in these petty, absurd political games, I think of you and remember the extraordinary courage, fearlessness, and dignity you demonstrated during your senate campaign in Nevada. That truly required strength, willpower, and . . . guts! Your courage is founded on accepting your condition as a foreigner, speaking imperfect English, a woman of color, and thus choosing a life of social activism, defending human rights and the edification of peace. I am more and more convinced that peace is a process that is becoming more powerful, day by day, and that requires construction, obsession, concern, and ceaseless effort.

What happened to me reveals a lot about the situation in the United States, where politics determines our morals, where truth and lie are confused. As you know, the controversy about Rigoberta has grown enormous. They're accusing her of being a supporter of a communist regime and a guerrilla, but the most serious matter is that she is accused of lying. Can you imagine?

Lie about her own history? An ultra-reactionary movement, motivated by the publication of David Stall's book, is accusing her of having lied about the facts of her life. The accusations are so harrowing because they say that her brother was not burned alive, but rather killed by the police. Can you imagine, Emma, writing pages and pages about one small detail when Rigoberta was trying to communicate a greater truth: that of her village, that of her people, the possibility of writing a profound, collective history that went beyond the barbaric details of individual deaths.

Emma, this country is so curious. They all live so obsessed to know the Truth . . . when the bigger truth is that the U.S. government and CIA are involved in the genocide against the native population, that is a truth that is strictly silenced.

And Emma, they have attacked me . . . vilely, rudely. I do not want to tell you all the details, because that would be to let them win, but I will tell you that the attacks against me have been ill-intentioned and detestable. They singled me out as the only woman who teaches about Rigoberta Menchu. They also said that I was Jewish and I had to teach in Brandeis University and all the attacks were focused in that direction. I believe, Emma, that history in the United States repeats itself and attacks us because we're women, because we're Jewish, because we're Latinas. All this is a paradox in a country that is seemingly devoted to promoting equality and democracy.

During this difficult time when I feel surrounded by evil, filthy gossip, the university administration has taken a noble, worthy stance and is defending my right to express my beliefs and to my academic freedom. Finally, after eighteen years, perhaps I am feeling more a member of this institution and not an outsider that's visiting Wellesley.

Dear Emma, I wanted to share this with you, for as little I've told you, so that you, too, can understand how I feel.

Your friend who loves you, your dearest friend,
Magi

✳

January 21, 1998
Reno, Nevada

Dearest friend,

When I returned from Chile, I heard the horrible news: my beloved city of Reno had been shaken by a tragedy. On January 7, as the sun was emerging from the mountains that surround our city, four men were torn apart in a devastating explosion that shattered the eternal silence of our desert. The explosion occurred in a factory where only undocumented Mexicans worked. They manufactured explosives by hand, and were paid for each one they completed—five or six cents per item. The faster they could make the explosives, the more money they earned. That morning, they came to work as usual, and a few seconds later their lives changed forever. Along with the men whose bodies disappeared, torn into small pieces scattered on the desert sands, some were very seriously injured, and others escaped with minor injuries to their eyes, ears, and skin.

This catastrophe made the public aware of the immigrant Latino's difficulties in this part of the country. They work, without papers, accepting whatever wage they can get. In this case, as in many others, they were not given instructions in Spanish, did not understand the risks of their employment, and were not provided adequate protection from the dangers of their workplace.

Like many of the immigrants that live in our community, these men were in a precarious situation, and worked from sunup to sundown to save a little money and send it to their families, hoping to return to Mexico someday, to their own house or business, or a little plot of land on which to retire. But destiny led them, instead, to this misfortune. The men who were killed left eight children without fathers, children condemned to a grim future. Some of those who survived had been in the United States for years and their children were born here—those men had to take their families and leave because of the threat of deportation. They lost their jobs and houses, and carried their children to a country unknown to them . . . a country that these children, penniless and uneducated, will abandon someday in order to return again to the North.

The shattered bodies as well as the pieces they could find were placed in coffins, and with the money we managed to collect from the community the caskets were taken to the U.S. border. From there the families transported them to their *pueblo* for burial. All the victims were under thirty years of age.

This tragedy reminded me of the hardships endured by the Chilean women who lost their sons, husbands, fathers, and brothers during the dictatorship. After attending mass, I returned home and wrote my weekly newspaper column. I enclose a copy so that you can understand the sadness I feel right now.

Love always,
Emma

"THEY HAD NAMES, THOSE MEN KILLED IN THE EXPLOSION"

Tragedies have faces and names. Many thoughts crossed my mind during the mass last week for the families and victims of the Sierra Chemical explosion, but the one thought that came back to me time after time was a short poem I wrote for a different tragedy, in a faraway land, for a very similar group of people. In the seventies I wrote a poem for the people who were disappeared in Chile. The poem came to mind when I saw the family and friends of the people who disappeared in the desert of Nevada. *No, no, they are not numbers / they are not numbers / they are names.*

And yes, the people who disappeared in the explosion had names. The newspapers, the TV, the radio kept referring to them as "the four dead" or the "one body recovered and the three disappeared," with no names, but they had wives, children, parents and relatives and many friends who will never see them again. I don't want to dwell on what happened or who is to blame because that will come out with time and proper investigations. But I do want to put faces and names on the tragedy—like the names of Demetrio and Marcos, two brothers who worked for Sierra Chemical. The body of thirty-five-year-old Demetrio was found, not intact, but in a way that could be put into a coffin and transported to the coroner's office, to the funeral home, and to Saint Therese, the Little Flower Church. Demetrio's wife, who had arrived from Mexico a few days before, silently followed the coffin containing the remains of her beloved husband while coworkers and family and friends wheeled Demetrio Hernandez to the front of the church. She sat in the front row and cried, looking at the coffin during the entire mass. Before the ceremony ended, Bishop Phillip Straling took a small cross from the top of the coffin and put it in her hands. She pressed it against her chest as the last earthly symbol that had been close to Demetrio's body, and now will have to remain close to her and her five children.

Next to Demetrio's wife sat a shy, petite woman who looked at the ceiling of the church and then down to the floor, all the while crying, repeating the same movement during the entire ceremony, rocking back and forth. She was Marcos' wife, and Demetrio's sister-in-law. Marcos' body had not been found, so his wife and three children did not have a coffin to mourn over, nor a small symbol that had been close to Marcos in the last minutes of his life or to his remains after his death. They cannot confront the reality of his death because they have not seen his body without life. To mourn the death of our loved ones, we need to see the end of their lives, but for Marcos' family that will never be possible. Marcos' wife will return to the family in Mexico accompanied by her sister-in-law and the coffin of Demetrio that will be buried in his hometown. Demetrio's children will take flowers to their father's grave every year on El día de los muertos (The Day of the Dead), as is customary in our culture, but their cousins will look to the sky wondering where, in a faraway desert called Nevada, lie the pieces of their father's body, the father who went away north across El Río Grande in search of the dream of a better life for his family. And like the father of those children, Marcos Martínez (23), there are two more people who disappeared on January 7: Alberto Acosta (23) and Francisco Espinoza (28). All left their families and came searching for the same dream, up north, a dream that turned into a nightmare for their families. For them they will never be numbers, they will always be names.

"One View," *Reno Gazette Journal,* January 28, 1998

May 1998

Dear Emma,

I would have loved for you to accompany me to the Jewish cemetery in Prague. It is to date one of the most sought-after tourist attractions, but it sets me to wondering if anyone has really stopped to think about what life was like in this completely enclosed ghetto, fenced in like a small concentration camp. People marvel before these tombs that seem to be a Dantean spectacle or a bad Hollywood movie. The cemetery is in a small corner of the ghetto and is a tiny place, as if all the dead wanted to be gathered very close together. The Jewish presence in Prague goes back more than a thousand years and, since the beginning, Jews have been living in small ghettos, places enclosed by the others in order to pacify and contain those who are different. I imagine girls our age wearing yellow stars on their sleeves, sewn on tightly because it was very dangerous to go out into the street without a star, that precarious sign of difference.

I do not know why I am writing this to you and you should not think, dear Emma, that I am too sad and obsessed with this history. It is that suddenly I feel very fragile and incredulous, and I want to converse with you about the limits of cruelty: up to what point is it possible to place people in ghettos, contain them, kill them, and eradicate their names from the memory of the living as well as that of the dead? I am writing this because this cemetery brings me thoughts of other forgotten tombs in Pisagua and the common graves of the General Cemetery: the famous Patio 29 where we went with Violeta and thought that every one of those dead, so young, was each our own, belonged to us, and we would recover their memory, their names, and their history.

Dear heart, we should not be frightened before the genocide of more than twelve million souls, this cemetery of persecuted Jews that is now a national monument, because the same has happened in Rwanda and Yugoslavia, because in this same period, varnished with the unlikely layers of sanity and education, have occurred the most brutal murders in all our history, and through this history men have not learned about themselves.

Here, Emma, strolled Kafka, who has now become a national hero. Before, they persecuted him in Prague for being Jewish and speaking and writing in German. Emma, my dear, my beloved friend, illusion of all illusions, I miss you tremendously, and in moments like these I want to feel your presence. Do you remember when we left forget-me-nots and orange blossoms in the General Cemetery of Santiago, and I taught you the ancestral and learned custom of the ancients? I miss you today while I am here in the Jewish cemetery of Prague, where I do not know if the dead rest in peace. When you visit the tomb of Salvador Allende, remember my dead and put small stones on their tombs. Tell them that your best friend has taught you this, a Jew without a tail or horns. Also, walk through Patio 29 where the N.N.'s are buried and, yes, of course, please pray for them.

Marjorie

✳

August 1998

Dear Emma,

It is certain that the truth is circular and repetitive, that man's histories could be a chain of smoke in the palm of the hand. Perhaps fortune-tellers have the gift of predicting voyages, uncertain roads where one day we all arrive in search of an origin. We humans are obsessed with knowing who we are, where we came from, and tracing the origin of our names. I am in Prague again, dear Emma, and perhaps you recall when I wrote about the history of the immigrant girls, when I told you of the sudden arrival of Tamara and Silvia, my cousins from Prague, to our house. At this time I find myself in Prague. I brought my parents to celebrate their fiftieth wedding anniversary. I will always remember that date because of the founding of the state of Israel, and because my mother tells me that on their wedding day it rained mercilessly and she also foretold that her wedding dress would be burned up, housed in a basement warmed by memories. Happily, that rain also lavished abundance and happiness upon them.

I walk between the shadows and the minarets. I think about those men and women, exemplified by Tamara and Silvia who, motivated and enamored by the dream of peace, traveled all these streets and, suddenly, history usurped their memories, not allowing them to be more than girls from Prague who were then transformed into immigrant Jews in the New World, somewhat as we two feel now, but not as immigrant Jews but rather as Latinas. I remember Tamara and Silvia often. I see their faces on other women, and I also have the deep satisfaction of saying to you that when they attended the Hebrew Institute, about which I've told you so much, they were not treated cruelly but rather with a profound love, with a great tenderness prompted by knowing that they were girls who had lost a piece of those golden cupolas, and that they carried, within them, other tragic histories.

Dear Emma, it is not a coincidence that we are in Prague. As chance would have it, although it may be more than chance, my mother ran into her cousin Jan Lodding, who when he was little was not Jan but instead had another name, the name of a Jewish boy. He is the first cousin of my grandfather Joseph Halpern, and only since 1990 did we know of his existence. His eyes reveal his history and the audacities of death. He was held in Terezin when, on the second day there, his grandfather died and then his father died in Bergen Belsen. He was finally rescued on his way to Sweden, where he was adopted by a gentleman with the last name of Lodding, and Jan decided to withdraw and not to say, feel, or tell anyone anything. Now in Prague, he talks to us desperately and, like everyone who has lost their history, he searches for a name, truncated genealogies, imaginary and real family stories. Now his life and ours are filled with new family characters. He talks about what we have only read in books and magazines. He tells us of Prague, of those cousins that my grandmother always remembers, and he speaks of Terezin and the butterflies that he could never manage to see from his cells.

I listen to him. We are in the Pushkin Cafe, and I suddenly feel that at this encounter all our family voices have arrived, all the stories of the dead and the living, that Julia and Sonia have sat down at our table. Everything happened very suddenly because, in that very moment, while I thought of this, Silvia Broder appeared next to our table. She is the one that lived with us in Chile so many years ago, and we began to converse as if nothing could interrupt this marvelous flow of who we were and who we will be. I notice that my mother's face became ever more clear and luminous while we visited the splendid cities where the dead take communion with the living. When the universe was a hazy and frost-covered cell, when one survived by denying all demonstration of humanity, so only then did these relatives come into our lives and the world open up for us.

Magi

※

August 1998
Reno, Nevada

Marjorie, my old friend,

The beautiful bouquet you sent me and the note of congratulations were received after I became a full professor. Two other people in my department, Ted Sackett, whom I adore, and Louis Marvick, a professor of French and one of my favorite people, were the only ones who stopped and congratulated me. The rest were silent. Some said nothing out of genuine indifference, but for others their silence meant to express "I'll show you that Emma's promotion to full professor doesn't mean shit to me." Maybe they are right because now that I have what I've wanted throughout my career, it doesn't mean anything to me. It's like getting tenure. We work hard to get where we are, but then we look back and realize that we gave up so much and missed so many opportunities, and now it's too late. We have lost so many marvelous things in our struggle to maintain our academic positions, and now that we have them we realize they aren't worth anything. It only means a little job security and the hollow prestige of being an academician.

I've pondered my role as a Latina in the academic world in the United States. I entered this profession because, as you know, I am sincerely dedicated to teaching. Part of my life are my students, I want to guide them, inspire them, open their eyes to the real world, and teach them how to discover the unimagined possibilities that their future will bring. They have been, in part, my guides and my inspiration, and through them I have learned to see the world from diverse perspectives. They have made me the professor I am today. Because of them I wanted, and still want, to be a professor. Almost thirty years ago I began teaching, and my spirit is still enriched by what I learn from my students. But academic life is completely different from what we dreamed it would be. Few academicians seem to have any heart for teaching nowadays. In some ways, it's not their fault that they've adopted this attitude—the system obliges us to put so much emphasis on other areas of our work. If we don't publish a lot, if we don't give papers at conferences or participate in stupid committees, we can't become a full professor. Because of this, there are professors who are awful teachers, and they'll be the first to admit that they don't have any interest in teaching, but they publish hundreds of articles about the hidden message in Shakespeare's dramas, spend years writing about the same subject, and end up being full professors. How many people read those articles? Do students deserve to pay an outrageous tuition to be taught by those scholars who have no interest in their students? I don't have any solutions for this crazy academic system, but with the passing of the years, I recognize that someday we will have to decide to be either teachers, in the truest sense of the word, or scholars. We cannot continue punishing the students because of the goals this system has set for us — to be famous scholars and, if time permits, accidental teachers.

Well, Dr. Agosín, fellow full professor, nothing has changed for me since I've climbed this next rung in the ladder of success that is leading me somewhere special, a place I have yet to discover and wonder if it even exists. My university is more than one hundred years old and I am the first Latina that has become a full professor. There has never been an African American woman or a Native American female professor who has earned this title. For this reason I don't feel proud today, I just feel sad. I am very sorry that I was the first, that nobody has recognized the importance of minority women and their noteworthy achievements. How many women before us deserved this title and died without getting it? I am also sad because I feel so alone. I have no one with whom to share this experience, nobody else understands the victories and defeats that we women, as non-whites, experience on a daily basis in this land of opportunity.

Marjorie, I hope that we are able to open the door for other women, the women who come after us — I hope we can help them arrive to the place that we, stumbling and alone, have finally found ourselves. Let's never close the door to other women as the door was closed to us because we were women, because we spoke with an accent, because we were dark-skinned, or Jewish, or because we came from another corner of the world.

Professor Agosín, I toast you across the miles for your full professorship and for mine. A toast to both of us because what we longed for has come to pass, although it is not what we expected.

I send you a big hug and my love,

Professor Sepúlveda

September 18, 1998
Reno, Nevada

My dearest friend,

I was in my office reading my students' papers and writing my
weekly column for the newspaper. I just looked at the calendar
and realized it is Chile's independence day, so I put everything
aside and I'm writing you because I wanted to talk to you across
the miles, not only about September 18 but also about a thousand
other thoughts that have occurred to me today. Do you remember
the celebrations that would begin on each September 15? Do you
recall the sound of guitars and hearing our traditional song, the
cueca, everywhere you went? And the fireworks every night? The
rodeos in the countryside? Marjorie, these memories are starting
to fade after all these years far from our Chile. I don't know if
you're having a similar experience, but just as we would look forward to September 18 because it would bring with it the first blossoms and a little warmth, I have begun to look forward to the
fourth of July here. I do not know if it is because of the similarity
in the seasons, or if it is because the passing years have slowly distanced us from our past, if we have become accustomed to our
new world. My memories of our independence day festivities are
now so hazy that, for the past few years, I only recall the date if,
by chance, I glance at a calendar. This important date no longer
means what it did before. Now I mark my life with new dates, and
I am beginning to have a new collection of memories as an immigrant in this land . . . can this be what they call "assimilation"? Are
we from here now? Will there come a day in which we will forget
our origins, once and for all? And if that happens, where will we
be from then?

Marjorie, all these questions come to mind now because, as I
told you on the phone, I keep getting insulting, sometimes threatening, letters and phone calls about my Sunday column in the
local newspaper. I finally felt, or perhaps only wanted to feel, that

I belonged here, and so in my column I began to defend the rights of Latinos in my community . . . and the thanks I get are miserable attacks in which they tell me to go back to my "own country." Which is my country now? Are we women without a homeland? Displaced forever and ever? Perhaps we must finally accept that being an immigrant means perpetually living in another's land and speaking their language, but that we will never think as they do. But we must also accept that, looking at who we are now, we can't go back because, after twenty-six years, it would be even stranger to return to Chile. We are simply from nowhere . . . but I prefer to be optimistic, and so we are from everywhere, too. And that is what inspires me to keep trying to save the world. The difference is, now I have to save the entire world, not just one country—just like I wanted to do when I was twenty years old!

I'll talk to you soon, my dear friend.

Emma

✳

January 1999

Dear Emma,

It was wonderful to see each other in Chile with our children. There is a phrase you use that has been etched in my memory. I feel your presence and hear your voice when I remember how you told me the following: "Every time, I am sorry when I say farewell to Chile, that I must continue saying good-bye to our dear home-land." Perhaps saying good-bye is a way of wanting to stay, of continuing the constant re-encounters with our homeland, as if it were a flow of voices and words. We have said good-bye to the Chile that was, to the Chile that changed drastically. The fissures on its face have made it a hazy and perplexed Chile.

In order to survive we invented a homeland for ourselves, and we rescued ourselves creating the kingdom of our childhood. Now it is our children who live in that kingdom, and thus we bring them here each year, so that they may always safeguard in their eyes the Pacific Ocean and the Andes mountains, so that their little bodies may be populated by fleas and caresses.

As you might have realized, my grandmother already had her ninety-first birthday, and she always remembers you for the sound of your laughter and the delicious, expensive chocolates that you bring her. I still like to hear her recall, with the astonishing clarity of the elderly (although she forgets superfluous details), her journey on a mule across the Andes mountains or the day she met my grandfather, the Viennese, in the Paseo de los Ingleses. She is also able to enumerate all the hills of the city of Valparaiso. It saddens me deeply to witness the loss of her sight and her hearing, but she is no longer interested in hearing everything and from her deafness has made another realm for herself. The same way you and I did with our memories.

It was difficult at the beginning to become accustomed to the mediocrity of the people in Chile. The dictatorship transformed us into beings marked by despair. Little by little we have been inhabited by large and small fears. Distrust has made us a nation of selfish beings.

I miss dearly what before was so pleasant, like the constant conversation, the peaceful dawns, and dealing with our countrymen. Nothing of this has remained. Nothing remains united. The country has not been divided because of the politics but rather because of the frustrations of daily life, the lack brought on by a poverty increasingly more unjust, and the hopelessness.

Only recently did we again become a people, appearing everywhere in the news as a confused and secret country, a nation distinguished by its fascism. All that saddens and stuns me, because this is also a land brimming with virtues: the women who unconditionally love their children, bless the daily bread, and live a life of especial subjugation. It is all that which I love, and also my Aunt Lucha, who directs the world from her wheelchair, and my uncle San Gollo, who sympathizes with his enemies and who still fixes the teeth of the humble people free of charge.

I have not seen many figures of contemporary literature, but they also form part of the dangerous structure. They lose themselves in the dark desire for fame. I will tell you something marvelous: when the plane was landing and I was preparing for the arrival that always fills me with complex emotions, I heard, like a loud hum in my ears, the voice of Gabriela Mistral—old, young, beautiful, divine Gabriela whispered in my ear. I wanted to be near her, to love her above all things, because she meant to tell me something, communicate very intimately with me, and to say: "This, too, is your land."

I'll see you in Arizona or call you. I've been asked to give a presentation at a conference of the Circle of Israelites of Valparaiso that my grandfather founded. As you shall see, history repeats itself, for I am to speak about my grandparents' arrival to the port of Valparaiso, a city where one never truly arrives yet always returns.

Marjorie

June 1999
Reno, Nevada

My beloved friend,

Having to write more than 500 words each Sunday for the local newspaper about Latino issues in the United States is more challenging than I ever imagined it could be. Especially for a simple woman who teaches in a state university, is raising a family, and struggling to survive menopause—while also trying to change the attitudes of a city that clings to the past, sometimes forgetting to open its eyes to the future. Marjorie, writing a column has been an enriching experience, often disheartening, but always intriguing and challenging.

As you know, I've taught at the university since the seventies and I have had more students than I care to remember, but I was not someone that people recognized across campus, much less throughout the city. I have written several books, and some of them have my photo on the cover, but that didn't even make people notice me. When I was running for the Nevada senate, in that bitter campaign, my face was plastered on billboards, smiling from the television screens, and photocopied on flyers that were delivered door to door. Even with all that, the majority of citizens in my beloved Reno couldn't match my name to my face. But Marjorie, would you believe it, writing a column has given me such a high profile that it's almost more than I can bear. Everything I've said and done in my life up to this point seems to pale by comparison. The few words that are printed in the Sunday paper, and the visibility that they have afforded me, also seem to have created in me two beings: there is the Emma from before the column ("Emma B.C."), and the Emma who has emerged while writing the column.

Since I began writing for the newspaper, not a week has gone by that someone doesn't stop me at the supermarket, at my son's school, in the bank, even at the movie theater to ask me if I am Emma Sepúlveda. At first, the question would surprise me, but over time I became used to answering with a simple "Yes." Yes, it's me, again and again, yes, that's me, repeating this affirmation . . . and I was again surprised when it dawned on me that this was all people wanted to know. They just wanted to confirm that I was the person they knew from the Sunday paper. Nothing more, nothing less—and with that, they would go on their way without another word.

Another group, a little more aggressive, surprises me in other, unexpected places—public bathrooms, at the hairdresser, or will stop me while I am running, unconcerned that I am sweaty and panting. They ask me if I am a member of the city government or a news anchorwoman. Of course, I say no and try to make my escape but, Marjorie, these people follow me and insist that they're sure they've seen me somewhere, and are determined to pester me until they can recall who I am. It is often impossible to extricate myself diplomatically from these situations, and I often end up telling them something like: "Perhaps you've read my column in the local newspaper." Their response to this always embarrasses me, because they are terribly disappointed, thinking they had seen someone famous, so our conversation ends with them saying something like: "Oh, is that all you do? I'm sorry, I had you confused with somebody important."

The people who interest me the most are those who stop me and ask me about specific columns. Sometimes they agree with what I wrote, sometimes they do not. I like these people for a variety of reasons. At least they recognize who I am and know I write a column (instead of thinking I might be familiar because I'm a stripper in one of the casinos!). These readers are interested in what I have to say, and they tend to offer excellent, intelligent comments in favor of or against what I have written. Thanks to these people I have learned to value dialogue, the communication that bonds a columnist with her readers. We dialogue at a distance. A lot of people have told me that they have cut a favorite column out of the newspaper and kept it, taping it to their refrigerator or to a wall in their office, or that they sent it to friends or relatives somewhere else.

When the column first appeared, something funny happened. A lot of my friends, colleagues, and students didn't realize that it was going to be a regular column, so they sent me cards and notes to congratulate me for having something printed in the newspaper. Each one of these well-wishers also sent me a copy of the column. Well, they eventually realized that it was a regular column and that I probably had a copy of what I had submitted to the newspaper . . . but not until I had boxes and boxes of cards, clippings, and extra photocopies of my own columns! Oh, and there were others who thought my column was a letter to the editor or newspaper, and they complained that Emma Sepúlveda's letters always got published but that the letters of other readers were ignored!

Now, most readers are accustomed to seeing my face in the corner of the last page of the newspaper. There are those who will always disagree with my commentaries and hate everything I write. There is another group that apparently enjoy my columns and agree with some of what I write—don't get the impression that they love me, but at least they don't tell me that my column is a piece of shit. And the last group, I believe (maybe just to bolster my own doubts because I think it's the majority) don't care what I write, it doesn't matter to them in the least. They don't love me, they don't hate me—they just haven't realized I exist.

This long answer is in response to the innocent question you asked me last time we spoke on the phone: Emma, what is it like to write a column for the newspaper? Did I give you the answer you expected? I don't know, my dear friend, I can only add that it cannot compare to writing poems, novels, and essays.

A big hug and, as always, all my love.

Emma

✳

January 16, 2000
Patagonia, Chile

Marjorie, my friend forever,

Here, at the end of the world, night has not yet fallen. The clouds are like fiery banners that wave victorious, whipped by the furious winds that sweep between the immense open sky and the magnificent Andes mountains. I love this landscape. When I visited last year, when I came to this corner of our Chile, I respected the custom of the natives of the region and ate the fruit of the *calafate*, and that is why I have returned. They say that all who eat of the *calafate* will return, and I now feel that this bewitching land has trapped me in its spell, and I am fated to constantly return to it.

Marjorie, there is nothing but silence in this faraway land, and the long, slow days come and go, causing me to forget the insurmountable reality of time. I walk for hours, following the narrow paths that have been tenuously delineated on the green hillsides, along the shores of the lakes, and the banks of the rivers that course freely down the rocky mountainsides. Here, all the earth is in harmony.

In Patagonia, Nature dresses herself in her best colors, she has invented sounds and aromas so that life will flourish in this blessed land. It is She, not man, who rules this region. And silence dwells here . . . it has invaded this lonely place, and one is truly witness to the indescribable presence of pure and immeasurable silence. At the end of the world it seems that time stops, and life appears to us as if it were a photograph instead of a movie.

The wind is also alive, and is a constant companion in Patagonia. This southern wind is born of the violent forces of the Pacific and Atlantic Oceans; their energies unite at this point, crossing along the hidden crevices of the gigantic mountains, becoming a savage gale that sweeps the pampas, valleys, and rivers. Here, the wind is a being of flesh and blood, like the palpable presence of silence. The powerful wind transforms the lakes into oceans, churning their calm waters. Condors float along effortlessly because the currents carry them . . . they travel the secret and mysterious path of the wind, transported between cloud and sky, between past and present.

I am here in the year 2000, at the end of the world, accompanied by the silence and wind, reflecting on the past. I left Chile during another January in 1974, and now I have been away for twenty-six years. It is no coincidence that I returned this year to say farewell to this distant corner, just as I have taken leave of other places in my beloved Chile. But this year is different because another chapter of Chilean history has been written. And tonight, I contemplate those years, the mysteries of time, and my own wanderings. In Patagonia, I say good-bye to the dead and the living, and I also let go the hope of ever properly saying the good-byes that were denied me when, as a young woman, I was suddenly forced to depart. I say farewell to the mountains, the sea, and my people who do not want me to say good-bye because nobody wants to lose one of their own. And amidst all these good-byes, I think of you, Marjorie. I'm wondering if you're writing me now, or if you'll write me tomorrow from Wellesley; and I think of how our destinies changed on September 11, 1973, and again today with the results of this year's elections in Chile, elections that have made our dreams come true.

I could not vote today. I was only able to vote once in our homeland, when I was twenty. I would give anything to be able to vote again. I would have voted for Ricardo Lagos. I would have voted against laws that keep killing our women through illegal abortions, laws that won't permit a divorce or protect women workers. I would have voted in favor of the defense of human rights and the demands for justice from the military government. I would have voted the same today as I did almost thirty years ago.

I listened to the news about Lagos' victory, here, in Patagonia. At the end of the world, I was given a new beginning.

LETTERS OF FRIENDSHIP AND EXILE

Ricardo Lagos spoke from the glorious Alameda where Salvador Allende, thirty years before, had promised a better future for Chile. Although the new president didn't mention Allende in his speech, the crowd that gathered knew that his spirit was there, and the echoes of Allende's words could be heard in the night, and they filled the hearts of many Chileans.

It is now midnight, and I write to you while pondering the departures and returns, the silences of the past and the fierce winds of the present. In the solitary confines of Patagonia, my spirit is divided between what I leave behind and that which I carry with me from this land, between the life I love in my new country and the people and places I cannot stop loving in Chile. I wish I could have voted today, I wish I could return to Chile forever. But my life is not what it was in the seventies. My family, my son and daughter, and my new dreams await me on the other side of the mountains. In that distant and beloved country, where I speak the language with a foreign accent, I still want to change the world, and I have found new reasons to keep our ideals alive. In that country I am not Chilean, nor am I North American. They call me Hispanic but I'm a Latina. I will go back, Marjorie, after this night of silent debate. But when I go back, I go home. The United States sounds like home to me. The thought of returning to the U.S. gladdens me, in the same way returning to Chile used to do, all those years ago. And now I can go home happy, knowing that Chile has returned to the path that it left in 1973.

I knew that this year would bring my fiftieth birthday. But I never imagined that, at fifty years of age, I would look back and be thankful for every tear I shed, every moment of pain, as well as the years of profound tranquility and happiness with which I've been blessed. I also never dreamt that I would have this birthday while living in the United States, or that I would call a city in the middle of the desert my home, or that I would live among people who tell me to "go back to where you came from" . . . people who do not understand that everything I want, without a doubt, is no longer to be found here in my birthplace . . . I only want to be, forever, *there*.

From Patagonia, with love,
Emma

AMIGAS

EPILOGUE

I am writing from my house on the edge of a stormy sea. I remember the beaches of my homeland, and the first time I met my Emma. It is not true that the past fades and is forgotten; on the contrary, our friendship is a memory that is born anew each day. Many years have passed during our exile, and we have come to passionately love our beautiful new America, in spite of its contradictions. But we have also guarded our Chilean childhoods as our most precious treasures.

Here at Wellesley College, I have been teaching about Chile for more than nineteen years, about its culture and people, and the opportunity to teach others about our small country has kept me close to my origins. Teaching is sharing the world with our students—it has nothing to do with the pettiness of academia. I think of my darling Emma, and believe that she and I are happy now. My Emma is with me everywhere . . . I see her now in the soft monotony of the falling rain, and soon I will hear that she has come back to me from Chile. They have awarded me the Gabriela Mistral Medal of Honor. This recognition also belongs to her, to Emma. I am deeply moved that the award has Gabriela's name, that eternal wanderer, the defender of children and women— she who, like Emma, has accompanied me on this marvelous adventure that is life.

—*Marjorie Agosín*
Maine, August 2000

The years have passed and life has changed us. I want to believe that it was we who changed our lives over the past thirty years.

I now write about Chile from the Nevadan desert. Only occasionally do I visit the beaches of Chile and, when I do, I find myself with Marjorie.

As yet, I have been unable to visit my mother's grave, and I want to believe that I have forgiven my father. My children speak Spanish with me and dream about this country in the North, their country. My husband continues to correct my mistakes in English, and I continue as a political activist. I teach in a university that is just as white as it was in 1974, when I began here as a student. In the midst of all the departures and returns, I still visit the Chilean *arpilleristas*, I still work to give a voice to those in my community who would otherwise go unnoticed, and I write to Marjorie every chance I get, from wherever I may be. I write her because I must describe in writing the friendship and love that has endured the test of time, of religion, dictatorship, language, and children. Marjorie answers me and we continue our ceaseless dialogue that binds us and unites us with our past and present; the crossing of our letters, back and forth, weaves the fabric of our lives as immigrants in the United States.

I have seen victory and defeat, and I like to think that I've felt more happiness than disappointment. And although many believe that I am not from here nor there, after all my experiences I can say, with absolute certainty, that I am truly from every place that destiny has carried me.

—Emma Sepúlveda
Nevada, August 2000